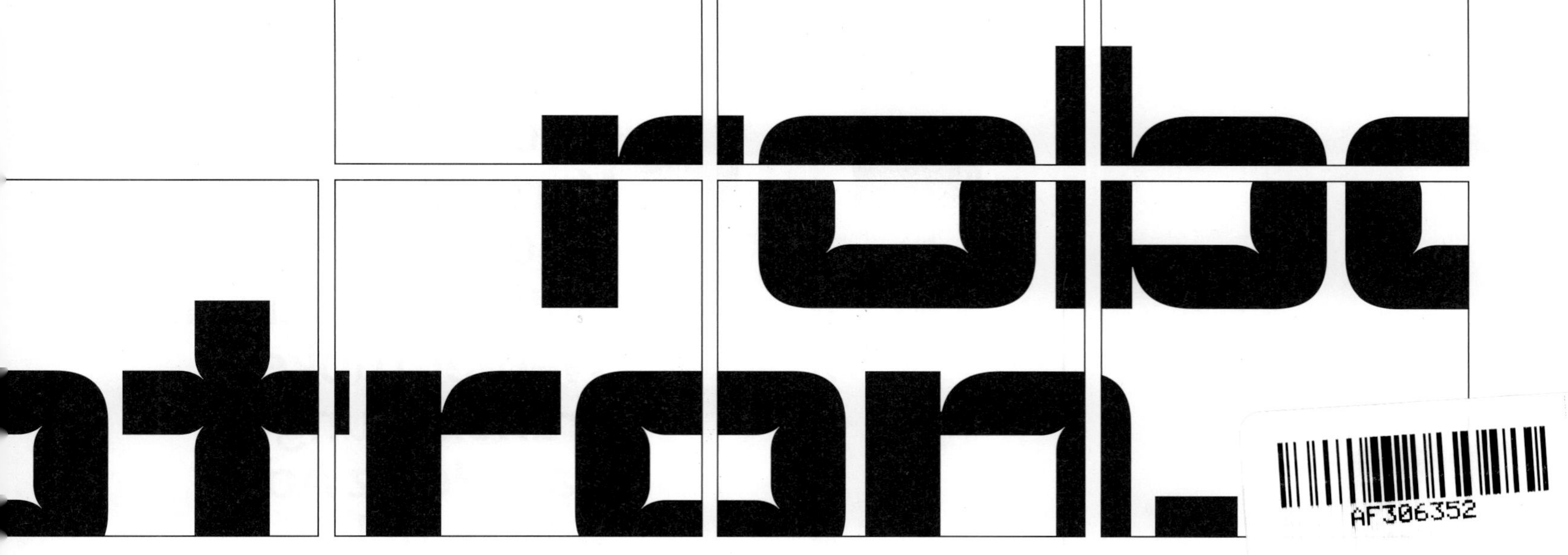

# robotron.

The publication accompanies the exhibition

Robotron. Code and Utopia
GfZK – Museum of Contemporary Art Leipzig
25.10.2025 – 22.2.2026

Robotron. Working Class and Intelligentsia
HMKV Hartware MedienKunstVerein Dortmund
14.3. – 26.7.2026

# Code and Utopia

Spector Books

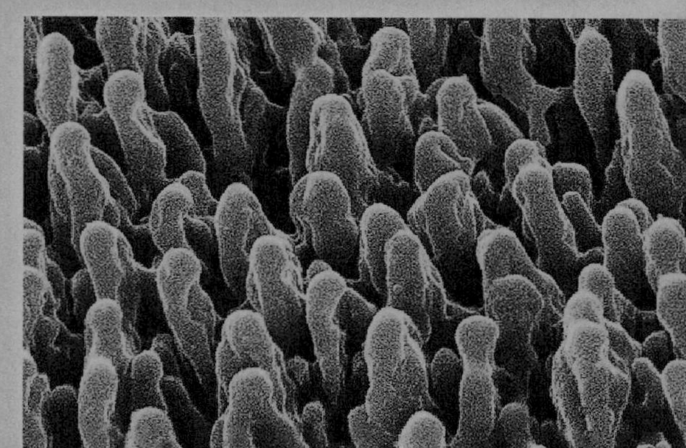

The term 'third industrial revolution' describes the profound transformations in all areas of work and life driven by the introduction of computers, automation, and information technologies since the late 1960s. The first industrial revolution, sparked by the invention of the steam engine in 1784, was a revolution of energy transformation. The second industrial revolution, beginning with assembly-line work and mass production in the late 19th century, was a revolution of labour organisation and distribution. The third industrial revolution, in which we find ourselves today, is a revolution of information. Depending on when one was born, one either remembers a world before this revolution – without computers, mobile phones, the internet, and 'intelligent' machines – or has grown up with them, immersed from the outset in a new reality. For the GDR, Robotron was to open the door to this third industrial revolution. In pursuit of this aim, the state invested enormous portions of its budget during the 1980s, yet it failed to keep pace with international developments. Ultimately, despite considerable effort, the GDR collapsed economically in the face of the third industrial revolution.

# Code

The VEB Kombinat Robotron (an industrial combine, or state-owned conglomerate) was established on 1 April 1969. The enterprise was headquartered in Dresden, with production facilities spread across the German Democratic Republic (GDR). The combine was responsible for the development, production, and distribution of electronic data-processing systems, small and microcomputers, process computers, control computers for telecommunications switching systems, and the associated operating systems and software. With around 68,000 employees and an annual turnover of 12.8 billion East German marks, Robotron was East Germany's largest state enterprise by the late 1980s. On 1 June 1990 it was dissolved, and the individual plants were converted into joint-stock companies with the Treuhandanstalt (the state trust agency responsible for privatisation during and after reunification) as their sole shareholder.

# VEB Kombinat Robotron

The dream of clear communication. A language without vagueness or ambiguity. Command language. The language of machines.

The development of computing technology in East Germany had several starting points. Before the Second World War, 80% of Germany's office machine industry was located in the area that later became the GDR. The most important production sites were in Karl-Marx-Stadt, Erfurt, Leipzig, Sömmerda, and Zella-Mehlis – cities that from the 1970s onwards also became centres of the VEB Robotron industrial conglomerate.

The concept for East Germany's first electronic mainframe computer, the Oprema, was developed in the late 1940s by Wilhelm Kämmerer and Herbert Kortum on an island in Lake Ladoga in the Soviet Union. The two Zeiss specialists had been compelled to work there after the war as part of reparations measures. When their assignments at Soviet research and engineering offices ended, they were required to remain on the island for another year. They were not permitted to take notes or scientific material with them when they left, which makes it difficult to reconstruct how much they knew about contemporary digital computer projects in the USA and the Soviet Union. On their return to Jena, however, they brought with them the idea for the Oprema. Built in 1954, it was East Germany's first programmable digital computer. The costs were high – the 17,000 polarised relays alone cost more than half a million East German marks – but the investment paid off after only four months. Although the Oprema never went into serial production, by 1956 the Zeiss ZRA1 automatic calculator was being manufactured on an industrial scale. This marked the beginning of the third industrial revolution in the GDR.

# Third Industrial Revolution

# What is Industry?

To imagine industry simply as a single factory is to think too narrowly, as though it were just one place where something is produced. Industrial production is networked – it forges connections between factories and people, their machines, skills, and knowledge. Industry denotes an interconnected mode of production, dependent on other processes, intermediate products, and factories. The effectiveness of this form of production depends not least on the reach and density of this network, and on its capacity to generate exchange.

## Groundwork for a History of the Third Industrial Revolution in the GDR

One must speak of technological innovations, research departments, and patents. Of the time required to take a prototype to the point of mass production. One must also consider the relationship between factory management and the Party, the hierarchies, party congress resolutions, and the dominance of politics over economics. One must examine the formation of combines – the consolidation of individual enterprises into larger economic units – and the questions of efficiency and governability raised by such vast structures. One must recall the Cold War, the trade embargo on key technologies maintained by Western states since the 1950s, and the attempts by the Ministry for State Security (Stasi, the East German secret police) to obtain knowledge and machinery clandestinely in order to close the technological gap. One must address levels of investment, the international division of labour, multinational capitalism, and failure to achieve independence from the global market. And one must speak of time itself – the pressure created by the dynamics of economic competition, where the truth of the adage 'life punishes those who come too late' reveals itself in its harshest form. All this must be considered if the disparate threads of reality are to be woven into a coherent history.

## Narrating the Economy

In 1929 Sergei Tretyakov proposed a new form of novel: the focus should not be on individual heroes but on things. The modern world, he argued, cannot be understood through the single human subject; economic processes, social relations, and the entire sphere of production cannot be adequately conveyed through the perspective of the individual. If, however, one were to follow things – from the extraction of raw materials to finished goods, from the factory floor to their circulation in the world – then human relations, with all their points of contact and conflict, would also come into sharper focus.

Applied to Robotron, this means tracing the origins of silicon and the production of microprocessors; the development of software together with the interplay of suppliers of components for computers; and the industrial espionage by the Ministry for State Security (Stasi) alongside the fragile sales markets for Robotron's data-processing systems in Eastern Europe.

The history of the third industrial revolution is also a history of an enormous, unprecedented concentration of capital. In the chip industry, investment costs rose by an average of two-thirds with each new generation. In its final decade, the GDR invested up to 30 billion East German marks in microelectronics – more than in any other industrial sector. For comparison: OpenAI currently spends roughly 30 billion dollars annually on the data centres for its AI infrastructure, far more than the entire cost of the Manhattan Project – the development and construction of the first atomic bomb.

# Nadja Buttendorf

rosie refers to a fictional merger between the GDR Kombinat Robotron and the tech giant Siemens: RO-SIE GmbH. Such a merger never actually took place. However, in February 1990, after the Berlin Wall had fallen and unification was imminent, employees of the combine suggested this name in the Robotron company newspaper. At that time, they were still hoping for unification on equal terms. Yet history took a different course. Nadja Buttendorf revisits the name proposed 35 years ago to speculate on an alternative future – one in which technological innovation is not driven by control and profit, but is able to realise its utopian potential. In her web series *Robotron – a tech opera* she explores computer development in a planned economy and the everyday life of female workers.

das Geschehen an
eine Videokamera
konnte man an ei-
das moderne Haus
tten (1400 Plätze)
einen Blick in ein
wofür pro Nacht

die Information,
kolade" mit Gun-
März ausgestrahlt
dabeisein konn-
11. März freuen,
locke im Speise-
ße den nächsten
nd, Stumphsinni-
schungen einläu-
**Günther Lotze**

n auf der Insel
21. leidenschaft-
talt aus „Cavalle-
ffnung, 27. grie-
Gewässer.

**Nr. 2/90**
ek, 5. Skalar, 9.
nara, 12. Rebus,
Etagere, 21. Blei,
Armee, 28. Ne-
, 35. Devise, 36.
senz.

Offen für Ei… …ichten, doch
vor allem de… …vergessen!

## Übrigens …

haben sich Mitarbeiter bereits einen Kopf über einen neuen Namen
für unseren Betrieb gemacht und würden, falls entsprechende Verhandlun-
gen z. B. mit Siemens erfolgreich ver-
laufen, als Betriebsnamen RO-SIE-
GmbH vorschlagen.

Herausgeber: VEB Robotron-Elektronik Dresden. Erscheint unter der Li-
zenz-Nr. 111 des Rates des Bezirkes
Dresden. Die Betriebszeitung „robotron" ist offen für den freien Mei-
nungsaustausch zu allen Fragen des
Betriebsgeschehens und der demo-
kratischen Erneuerung. Veröffentli-
chungen stimmen nicht in jedem Fall
mit der Meinung der Redaktion über-
ein …

kau… …
hat ihren …
nisse der …
tralmesser…
der Halle …
18. Robo…
mit seine…
des Mess…
**Von w…**
lungen w…
besonder…
Wir bi…
den inte…
grund ste…
messe v…
orientiert…
aus wes…
Wir rech…
tigkeit m…
tionsbezi…
durch, …
Koopera…
bringen, …
neue O…
Bedeutu…
stellt. W…
die trad…
stungen, …

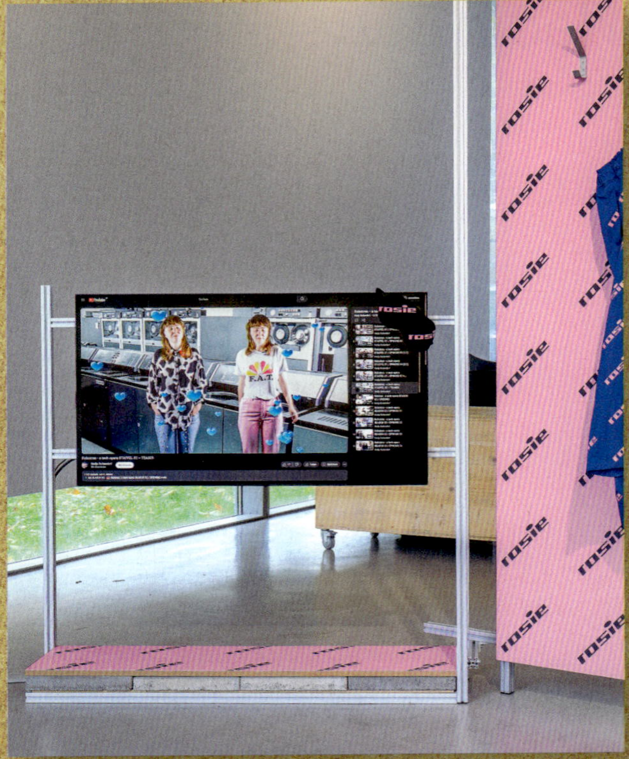

rosie
2025 | Word mark (design: David Polzin), pyjamas, sleep mask, excerpt from
the workers' company newspaper of VEB Robotron-Elektronik Dresden
and VEB Robotron Projekt Dresden, 14 February 1990, no. 3/90, last page
dimensions variable

Robotron – a tech opera, Season 3D (aka Season 04)
2021 | Video, colour, sound, 3D animation, 4K, 16:9 | 11:00 min

# Karl Clauss Dietel
# Georg Eckelt

Karl Clauss Dietel's (1934–2022) form and product design stands for the 'Open Principle': with his comprehensive technical understanding, he made the components and functionality of devices visible. Taking an interdisciplinary approach, he promoted the close integration of development, design, and production in his projects. In 1963, Dietel was commissioned to design the Robotron 300 mainframe. He collaborated with designer Christian Berndt on this project. Its presentation at the 1966 Interorgtechnika in Moscow was a major success. Although the R 300 was less powerful than contemporary Western mainframes, it was widely used across many GDR enterprises. For the documentation of the product, Dietel proposed the industrial photographer Georg Eckelt (1932–2012). From 1963 onwards, Eckelt worked for various designers, industrial enterprises, and the Deutsche Werbe- und Anzeigegesellschaft (DEWAG), the monopoly advertising agency in the GDR. His photographs highlighted design details and presented the R 300 as a modular and expandable system.

Robotron mainframe computer R 300, unknown photographer

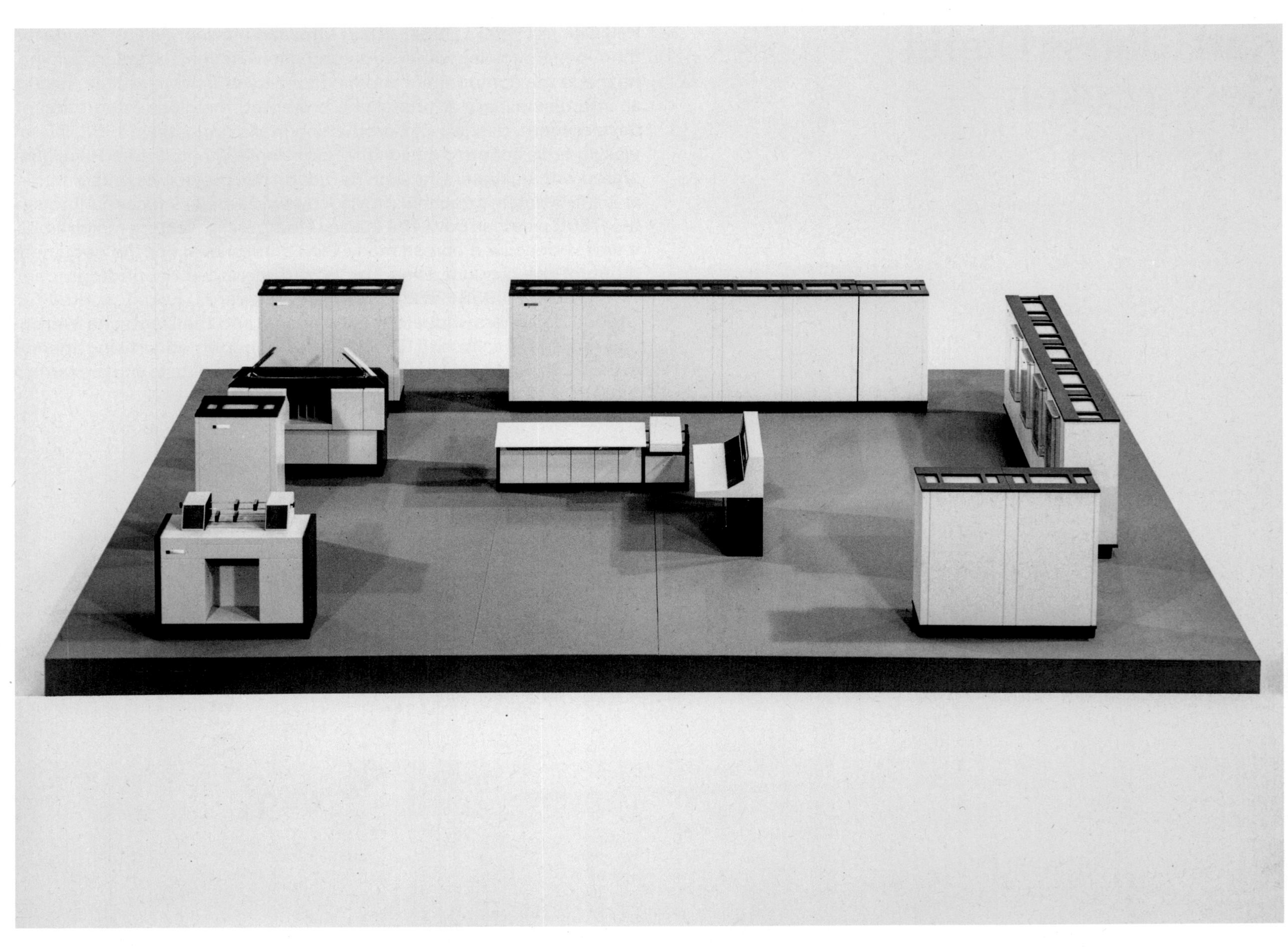

Robotron mainframe computer R300, model, photographed by Georg Eckelt

Cabinets of the central unit, photographed by Georg Eckelt

Robotron mainframe computer R300, unknown photographer

The philosopher William James, who coined the term 'pragmatism' in the late 19th century, answered this question as follows: 'there is at all times enough past for all the different futures in sight, and more besides, to find their reasons in it, and whichever future comes will slide out of that past as easily as the train slides by the switch.'

# Metamorphoses of Technology

How did a calculator or typewriter become a computer? How did the transition from mechanics to electronics occur?

The traditional production sites for office and calculating machines in Sachsen and Thüringen – Rheinmetall in Sömmerda, Mercedes in Zella-Mehlis, Astra in Karl-Marx-Stadt, and Optima Büromaschinen in Erfurt – proved in the 1950s to be more of a brake on the development of electronic calculating machines. From the turn of the century until the outbreak of the Second World War, these factories had held their own against strong international competition. The Archimedes, Continental, Mercedes-Euklid and Triumphator calculators, together with the US Hollerith and Powers machines, set the international standard for calculating machines. In the 1950s, their research departments worked on optimising electromechanical calculators, but the expertise and personnel needed for the electronic age were still lacking. Success sometimes also creates inertia.

# Control and Decision-Making

# What Is Planned Economy?

Industry in East Germany was organised as a planned economy. The political leadership and state planning authorities decided centrally on the development of individual sectors, the production and distribution of goods, and investment priorities. The model was the Soviet Union, where the socialist planned economy had been developed since the 1920s as an alternative to the market economy.

As a fundamentally new economic concept, the planned economy became a process of continuous experimentation – an attempt to discover how the economy could be planned and steered efficiently and centrally. This process was accompanied by many missteps and setbacks. In East Germany, too, the organisation of the economy was in constant flux: from its founding in 1949 until its end in 1990, it was continually being restructured.

Economic processes require constant adjustment and realignment. What is successful today may not be tomorrow. In the GDR, these steering processes took place primarily at the political level. At the Third Party Conference of the Socialist Unity Party (SED) in March 1956, held under the slogan *Modernise, Mechanise, Automate*, the leadership gave important impetus to the development of program-controlled computer systems (early digital computers). In his speech, Walter Ulbricht called for the 'attainment of world standards in as many fields of science and technology as possible' and insisted on the innovation and competitiveness of the East German economy.

Alongside new metallic materials, new plastics, nuclear physics, and the mechanisation of agriculture, semiconductor technology, process measurement and control engineering, and electronic computing units were among the priorities of the second five-year plan – and thus among the fields in which research and development were funded.

In the 1950s, the research field of cybernetics captured imaginations in both East and West. At its core, this new science – combining aspects of biology, linguistics, game theory, and more – was concerned with theories on control processes and information transfer. Automation and the prospect of machine learning were areas of application for cybernetics, but it also raised questions about the self-regulation of society and economic processes. How can systems be regulated and stabilised? How can information be stored and converted? How should information exchange be organised within a system, and between different systems? These were the problems cybernetics addressed as a theory of dynamic, self-regulating, and self-organising systems.

In the 1960s, East German political leaders saw in cybernetics, and its practical implementation in electronic data processing, an opportunity to put the planned economy on a scientific footing. As the daily newspaper *Neues Deutschland* wrote in March 1964: 'Only with the help of electronic data-processing systems can the complicated, interwoven relationships in our economy be processed in such a way that flawless, forward-looking decisions can be made. With electronic calculating machines, the planned economy finally receives the necessary technical foundation. Now planning can be significantly improved.'

The new idea was to view biological, physical, and social behaviours as programmed and therefore reprogrammable. The cybernetician imagines every behaviour as though it were ultimately 'steered' by the survival imperative of a 'system' – a system that makes this behaviour possible in the first place and to which it must contribute.

# Crisis and Balance

Cybernetics is a philosophy of equilibrium that originated in the crisis of the Second World War. The American mathematician Norbert Wiener, together with several colleagues, was commissioned to develop a machine capable of predicting and tracking the positions of enemy aircraft so that they could be shot down reliably. Wiener's insight was to translate the problem of uncertainty into a problem of information within a time series – one in which certain factors are already known and others not yet – and to view the whole as a 'system'. The solution lay in repeatedly feeding the deviation between the desired behaviour and the actual behaviour back into the initial conditions, so that the two converge as the deviation approaches zero.

The French biologist François Jacob reported that his investigations into cells had revealed a communication system operating between different molecules. This system ensures that molecules are informed at every moment of what is happening around them, enabling them to work in an extremely coordinated manner. As soon as one deals with systems, Jacob observed, one encounters phenomena of communication and control.

Alongside the rise of cybernetics, a way of thinking in structures and systems took hold in various scientific fields during the post-war period – in linguistics and genetics, but also in anthropology. A similar observation was formulated time and again: complexity arises through the combination of the simplest elements. The genetic information encoded in the chromosome consists of four elements combined millions of times over; in much the same way, information in language is encoded through the concatenation of a very small number of characters. To integrate these simple elements into a more complex structure, rules of organisation are required.

# What Is Cybernetics?

# Ruth Wolf-Rehfeldt

*Typewritings* was the name Ruth Wolf-Rehfeldt (1932–2024) gave to her typewritten graphics. From the 1970s onwards, she used the typewriter to arrange letters, punctuation marks, and words into images and geometric forms – sometimes in German, sometimes in English. She was part of the international Mail Art movement, sending her works from East Berlin to destinations across the world. They speak both of the constraints of life in a repressive state and of the Cold War, as well as addressing global industrial development and its consequences for the planet. Wolf-Rehfeldt was also interested in cybernetics and information theory. Her 'cubes', 'boxes', and 'cages' offer a criticism of the surveillance state, while also drawing parallels to computer technology – as in her series *Zeichenräume*, where she cites the binary code of ones and zeros, the very basis of digital information processing. In *Steps to Heaven (Steps to the Stars)* she extends her cubes into robotic figures, parodying notions of technological progress such as artificial intelligence and robotics as substitutes for human labour.

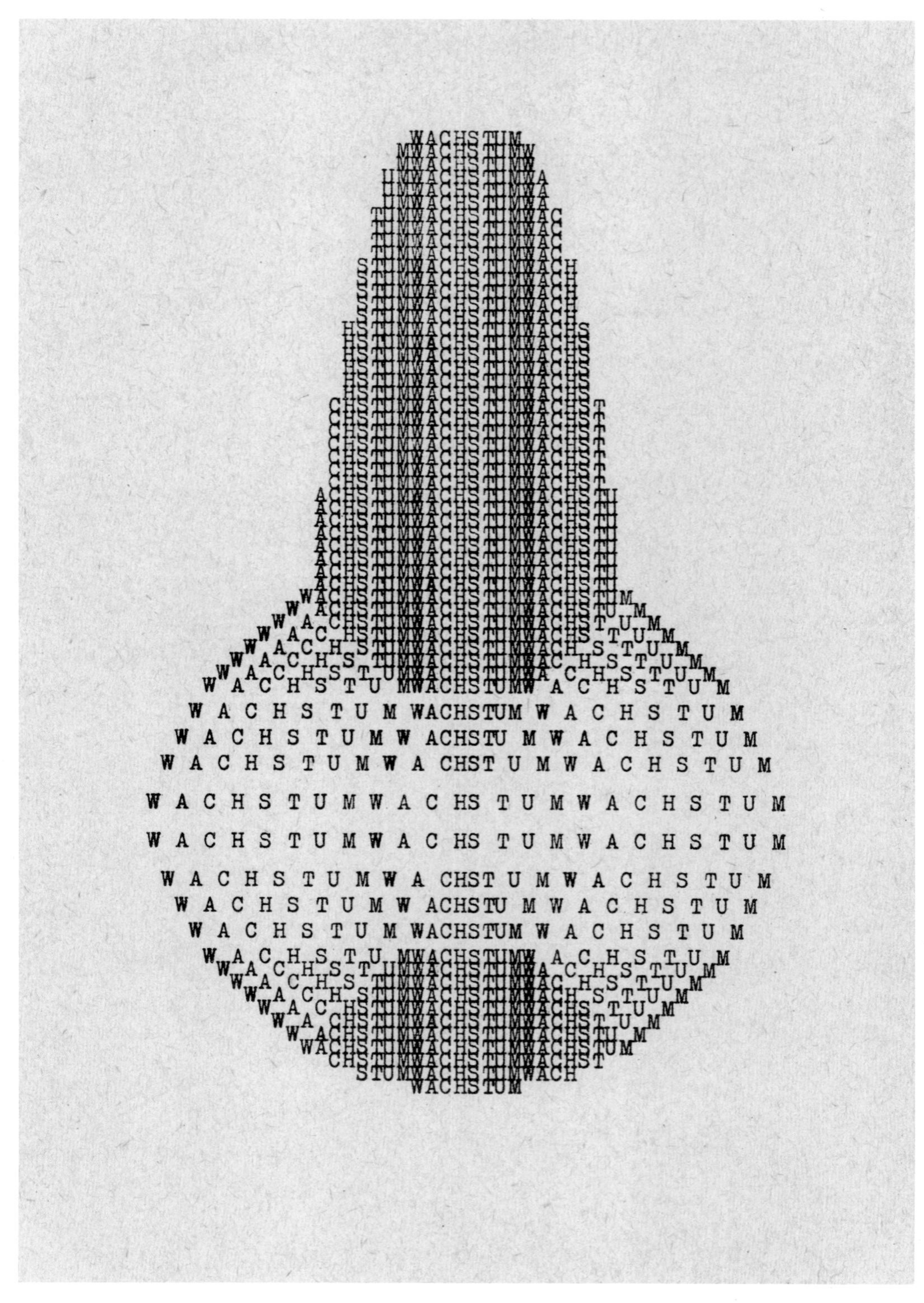

Wachstum (Growth)
1970s | Zincography | 21×14.5 cm

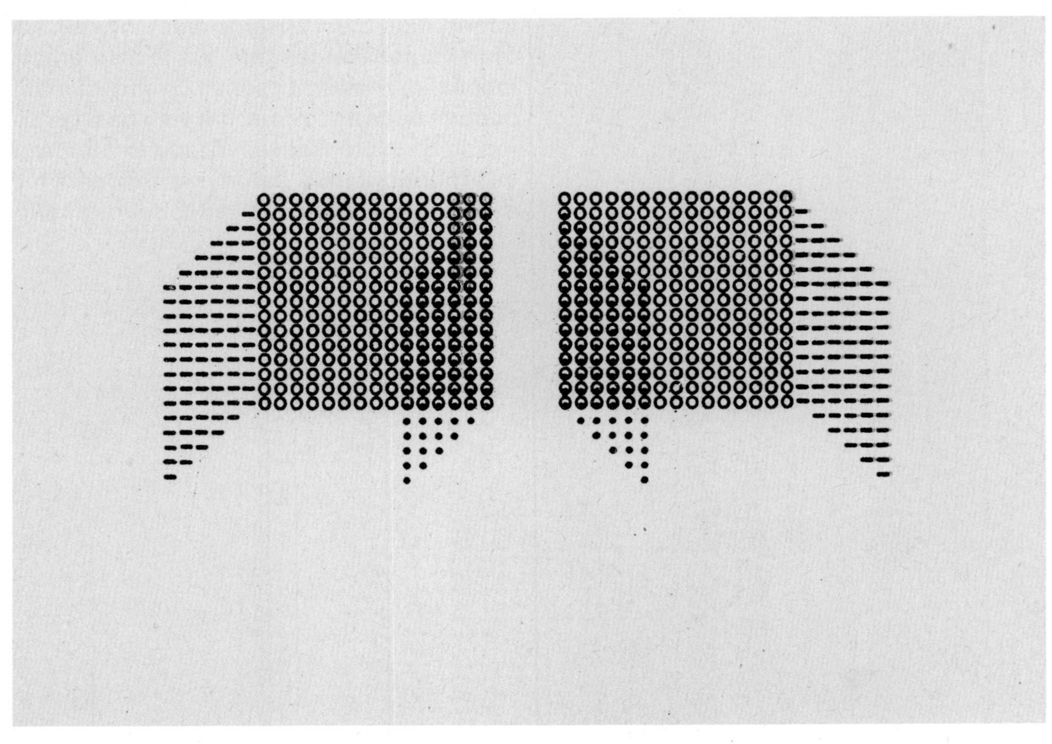

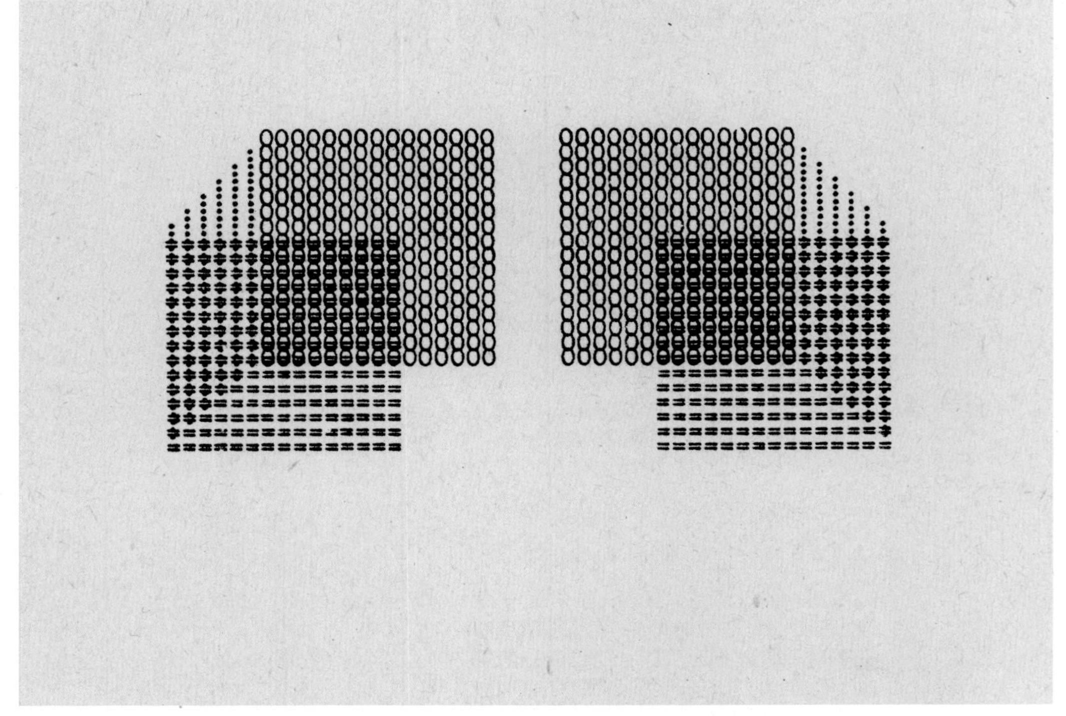

Zeichenräume (Cases and Cages)
1970s | Zincographies | 10.5×14.5 cm

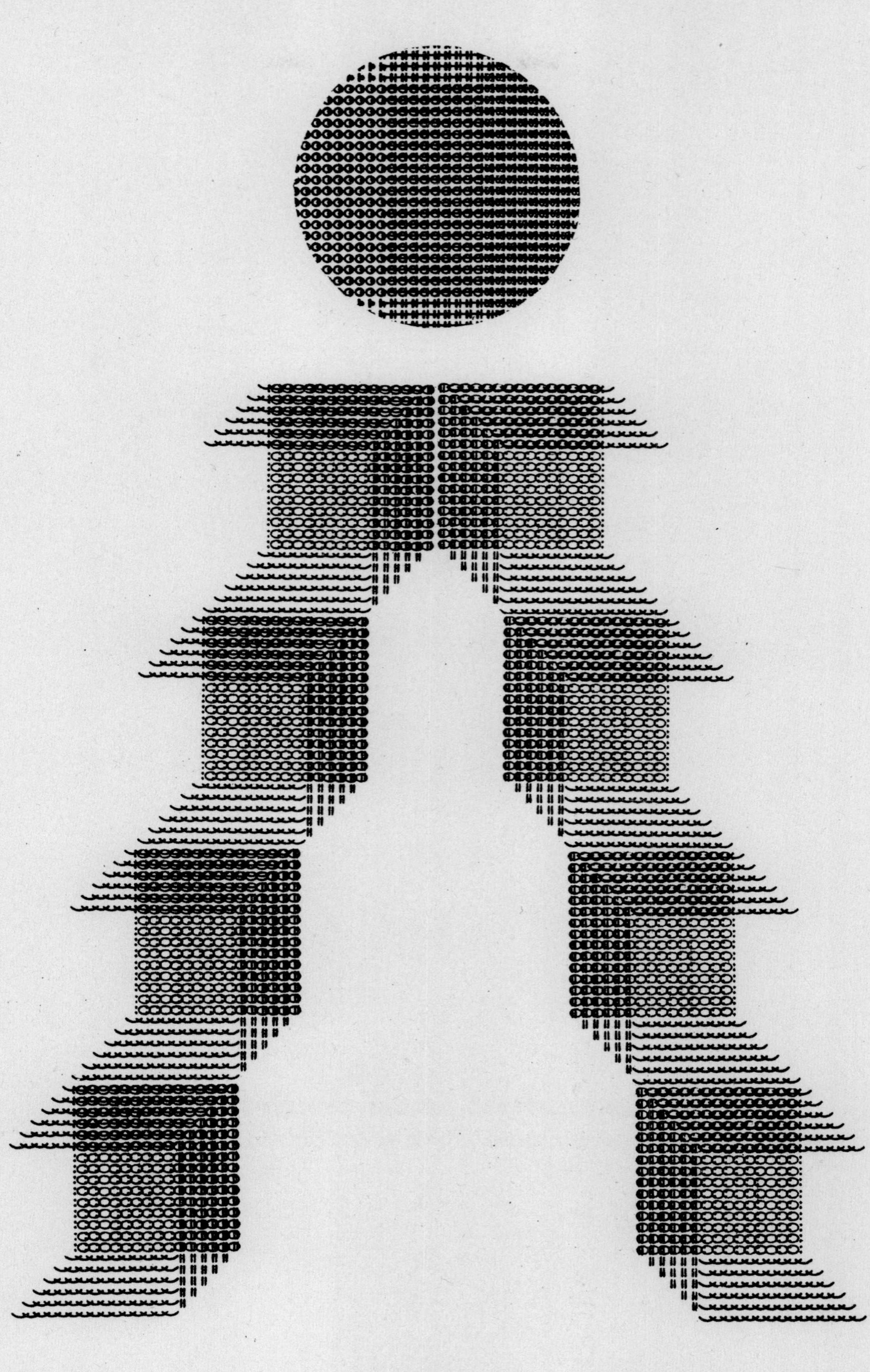

Steps to Heaven (Steps to the Stars)
1981 | Zincography | 31×21.5 cm

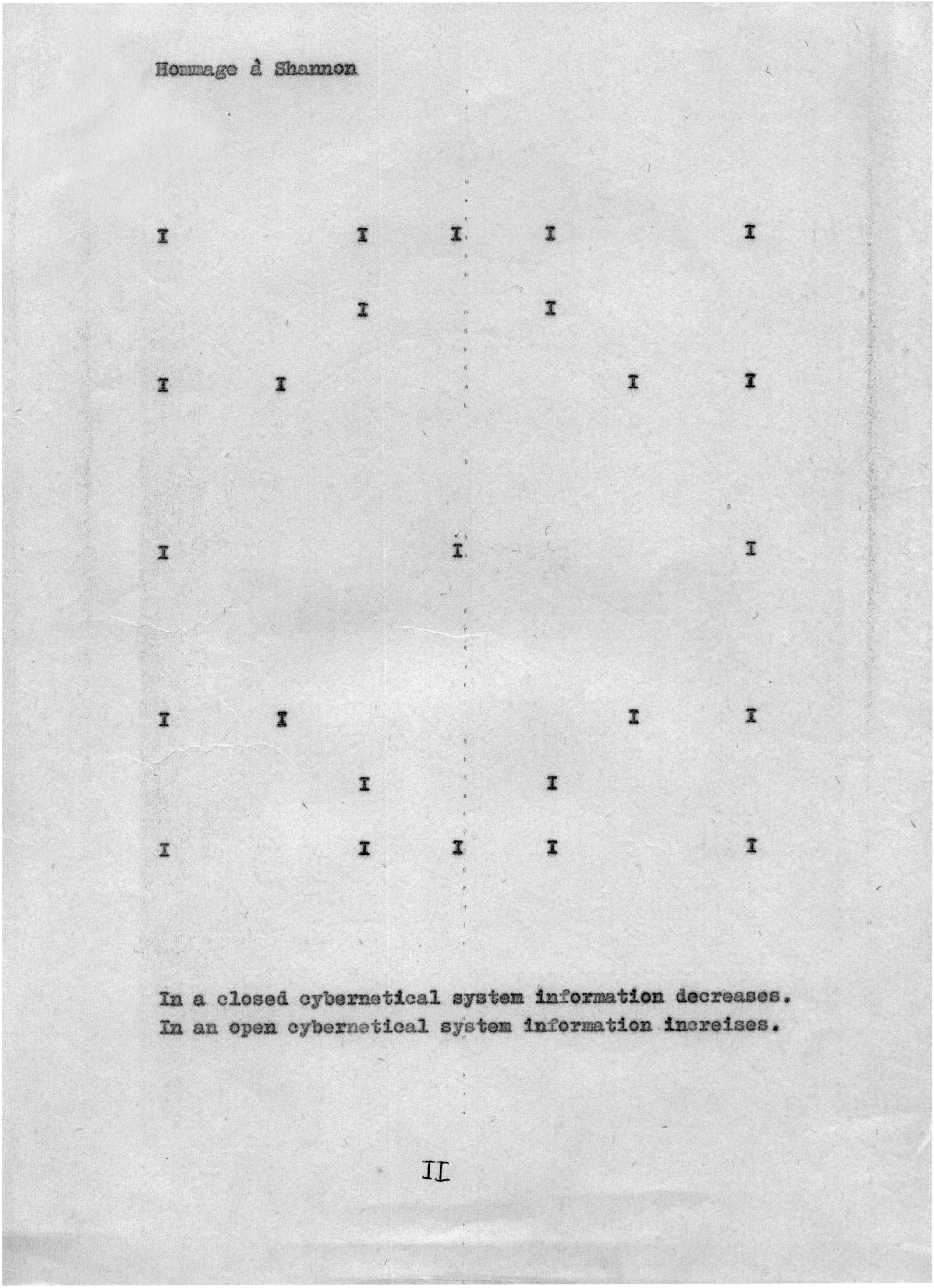

In a closed cybernetical system information decreases.
In an open cybernetical system information increises.

II

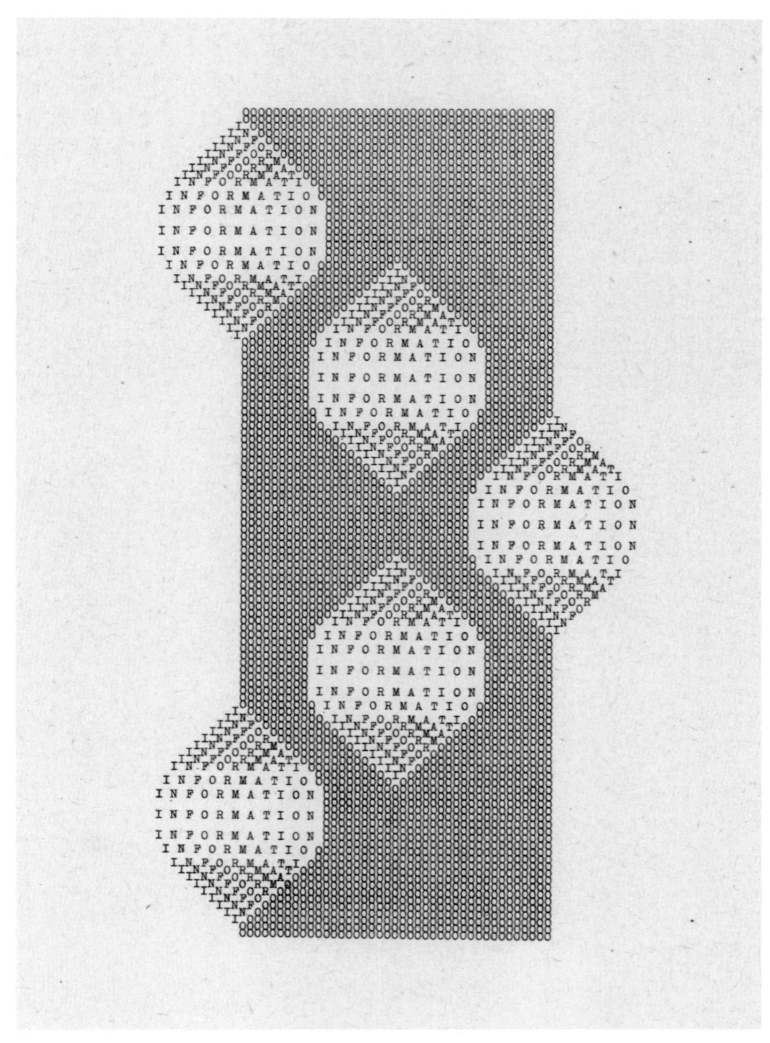

Information (Informationsbildung)
1970s | Zincography | 14.5×10.5 cm

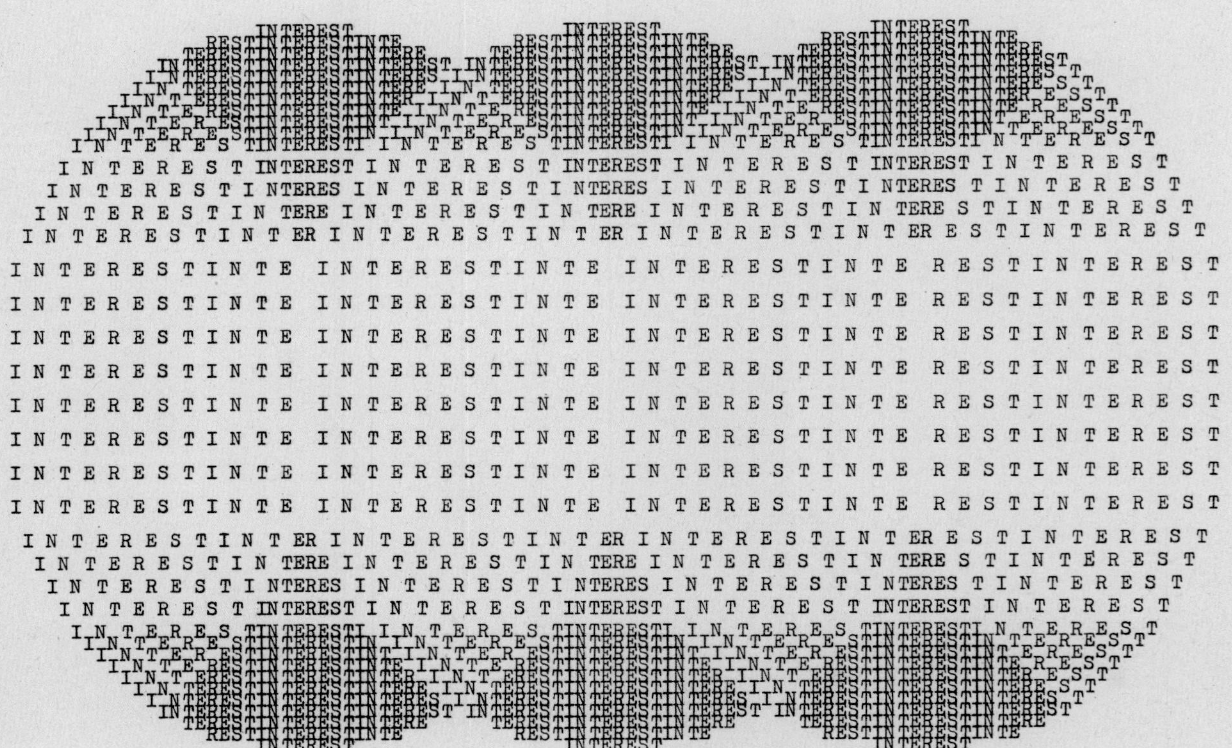

**Spheres of Interest**
1979 | Zincography | 21.5×30 cm

# Werner Tübke

In the early 1970s, Werner Tübke painted the monumental mural *Working Class and Intelligentsia* for the Karl Marx University in Leipzig, commissioned by the Socialist Unity Party (SED). It measures 270×1380 cm and depicts individuals, mostly real, who symbolically represent socialist society arranged in groups such as 'work' or 'family life'. The 'research' section is represented by a scene in which people are hard at work on a Robotron 300 mainframe computer, the heart of the university's computing centre. It was developed between 1963 and 1968 at the VEB Electronic Computing Machines Plant in Karl-Marx-Stadt, based on an IBM design. Tübke lets it shine above society – great hopes are invested in the possibilities of economic organisation supported by data processing. He produced numerous sketches and preliminary studies to accurately depict the control desk, punch card devices, and magnetic tape drives of the room-filling computer. After the demolition of the university building in the early 2000s, Tübke's mural was transferred to the new complex.

Computation Centre, preliminary study for Working Class and Intelligentsia
1971 | Graphite on paper | 65.8×95 cm

Arbeiterklasse und Intelligenz (Working Class and Intelligentsia)
1970–73 | Oil and tempera on fibreboard | 270×1380 cm

Installation view at the former main building of Leipzig University
2006

22

# For Cybernetics

Cybernetics is a massive evolutionary leap: the marriage of human and machine. Through it, humans can grapple with the complexity of reality, having understood that this complexity is controllable once it is grasped as a dynamic, dialogical system.

Cybernetics objectifies life, replicating it with ever-greater virtuosity in technical models. Even the human mind – for millennia a divine black box – can be broken down into a sequence of individual operations, into decision nodes and feedback loops. Thoughts, dissolved into mathematics. Delegable to computing machines that work faster and more reliably than humans. Where a person needs seconds or tenths of a second for a logical operation, these machines perform it in a millionth or billionth of a second. What acceleration, what a gain in time. And the machines are changing at tremendous speed. They are starting to learn, to react; they work autonomously. Humans will leave the fully automated factory, step out of the drudgery, the monotony of physical labour. Soon, monitoring – right down to the self-regulation of malfunctions and breakdowns – will also be automated. Workers in the true sense will no longer exist. The presence of humans in operating facilities is almost a disturbance.

The change that is ultimately decisive for individual life is the abolition of money, of private property, indeed of the concept of property; the abolition of public administration, and thus the elimination of any state order. The government of people by people has been replaced by the administration of things by things. For all administrative processes required for the self-regulation of production and distribution are handled by electronic data processing centres. Lifetime is no longer a commodity. With cybernetics, the prehistory of humanity ends and true human history begins.

Sputnik in 1957, the unmanned lunar landing in 1959, and Gagarin's space flight in 1961 generated a wave of technological euphoria that lasted throughout the 1960s and carried with it social expectations. The victory of socialism was regarded as a historical inevitability. Walter Ulbricht, who stood at the head of the SED Central Committee, was highly receptive to this euphoria. 'He possessed a faith in science that was astonishing for a politician and unusual for a communist functionary,' writes his biographer Ilko-Sascha Kowalczuk. Ulbricht grasped that science and technology in the second half of the 20th century were becoming 'more and more of an immediate productive force', which is why he counted the natural and technical sciences as part of 'the realm of material production'. He had thus understood a key dimension of the epochal upheaval that industry was undergoing in these years, and in his policies he sought ways to raise labour productivity through scientific, engineering, and organisational achievements, and to pursue reforms in the system of planning and management.

Cybernetics transformed not only the image of work but equally that of the worker. In 1966, the philosophers Georg Klaus and Heinz Liebscher wrote in their book, *Was ist, was soll Kybernetik* (What is Cybernetics, What Should It Be): 'At the stage of automation, the human finally appears as the constructor and supervisor of the control system.' In automated production, the old physical-mechanical labour gave way to the work of communication, steering, and control. The manual labourer became a guardian of the production process, entering into symbiosis with the technical apparatus: the male worker at the control panel, the female worker at the mainframe computer or microscope. Although the visual inventions in the works of A. R. Penck and Werner Tübke appear completely contrary, the impulse driving their work in the late 1960s was the same: they depict the human being in the third industrial revolution.

# The Utopian Decade

Until the late 1940s, East Germany's office and computing machine industry had no link to a university chair in a technical field. This lack of academic research delayed the development of mathematical theories of computing that could have led to program-controlled digital computers. Such research began only in the 1950s and led in 1956 to the founding of the Institute for Computer Engineering at the Technical University (TH) in Dresden. At the same time, Dresden – the capital of Sachsen – was the centre of the GDR's aviation industry. When this was abruptly shut down in 1961 due to lack of demand, the state leadership sought to prevent aviation experts, highly qualified electronics engineers, and automation specialists from moving to West Germany. In the 1960s, Dresden was therefore made the centre of the East German computer industry. The scientific prerequisites were already in place.

# Kairos not Karl Marx

The Robotron 300 data processing system was developed at VEB Elektronische Rechenanlagen Karl-Marx-Stadt. The design was completed in 1964 and presented to the public for the first time at the Interorgtechnika exhibition in Moscow in 1966. For the trade audience, it was a sensation that demonstrated the independence of East German industry. 'It was something unique within the limits of our possibilities,' recalled the product designer of the R 300, Karl Clauss Dietel.

Between 1968 and 1971, around 350 units of the R 300 were produced – a large number for the time. The system cost 3 million East German marks and was usually operated in a three-shift system because of its high expense. At least eight people were required to run it: a shift supervisor; first and second operators, both double-staffed; a magnetic tape archivist; and several system technicians. The R 300, with its 45 cabinets, required an installation area of 35m².

# Robotron 300

The introduction of electronic data processing in East Germany was delayed in the 1960s, and the gap with the western industrialised nations grew. There were several reasons for this. Budgeted funds were insufficient, meaning many projects could only be realised slowly. Not all production fields developed at the same pace. When the production samples of the R 300 were ready in 1967, some peripheral devices could not yet be delivered. The delays also meant that no test machines were available for a long time, even though software could not be tested without the computers for which it had been designed. Another problem was the lack of specialists. The State Secretariat for Higher Education was inadequately prepared for the requirements of the data processing programme, and companies were not made ready in time for the use of data processing systems. Telling in this regard is the remark of the head of computer centre at the Berlin light-bulb factory, who recalled that the preparations for electronic data processing had been made without ever having seen the relevant computer or having any information about it. Development was also slowed by the lack of advance research, as the funds available for this remained below international levels. Work on the successor to the R 300 therefore progressed slowly, and it was not presented to the public until 1972. A further drawback was that, with East Germany's increasing isolation, most scientists and engineers were excluded from international information exchange. All this led to a loss of valuable time: by 1970 there were already about 80,000 computers in the USA, around 6,500 in West Germany, and only about 630 in the GDR.

# What Is Progress?

# Francis Hunger

Using historical film footage from the House of Statistics in Berlin, Francis Hunger explores how bureaucracy, statistics, and computer technology shaped everyday administration in the GDR and were reflected in the language of socialist discourse. The term 'hypnagogia' in the title refers to a state of consciousness in which visual, auditory, and tactile hallucinations can arise while falling asleep. Cumbersome bureaucratic terms echo throughout the video, in sharp contrast to the contemporary cityscape at Alexanderplatz. In the GDR, almost all procedures, institutions, and legal frameworks were based on statistical data. To this end, the State Central Administration for Statistics and the Central Office for Primary Documentation were established in the House of Statistics. Here, the State Planning Commission worked on the implementation of socialist economic planning goals within a five-year plan. The audio track of Francis Hunger's video installation is based on legal texts from the GDR that describe the role of statistics in relation to economic planning and electronic data processing: procedures, institutions, and legal frameworks.

Statistical Hypnagogia
2021 | Video, colour, sound | 12:26 min

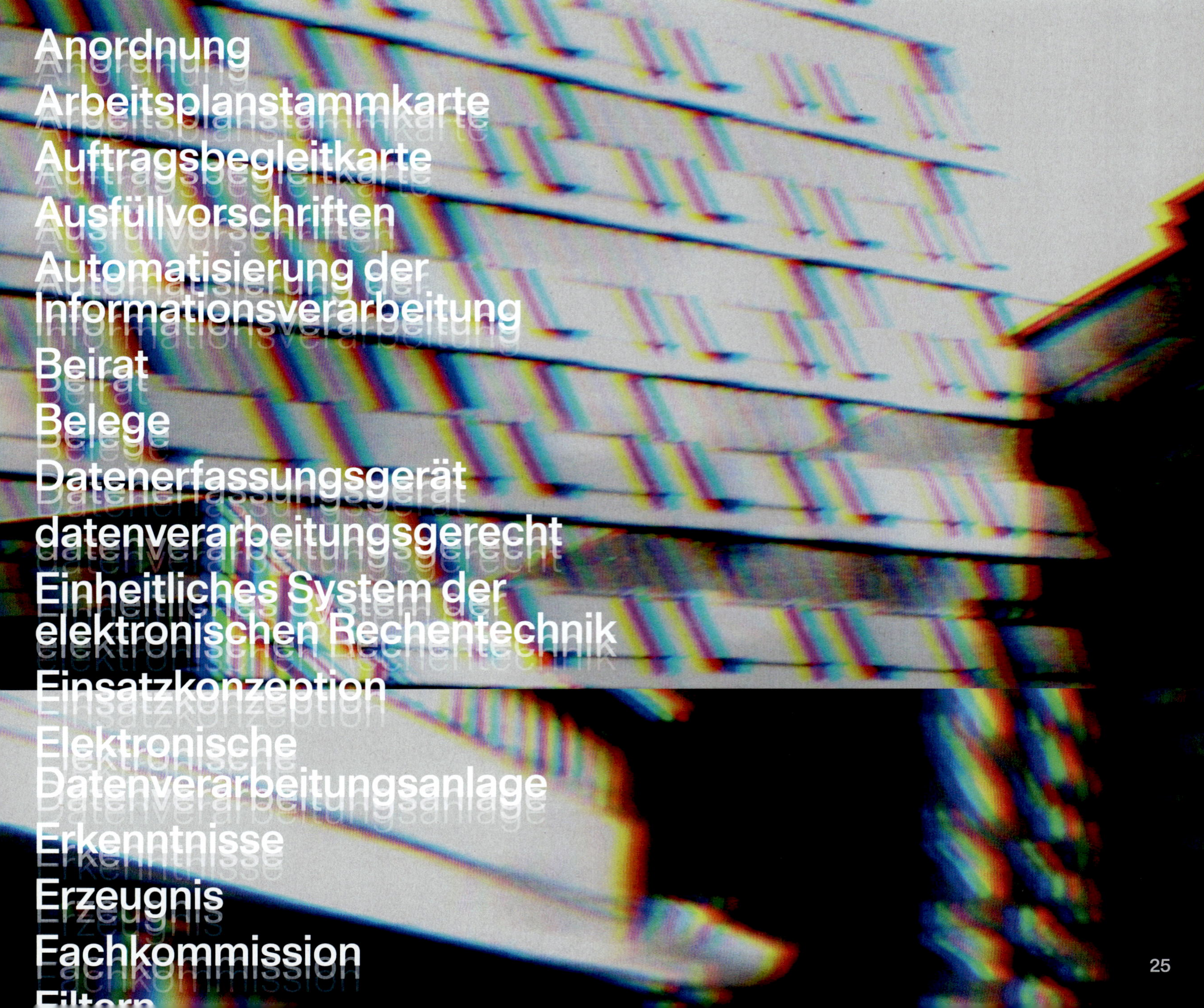

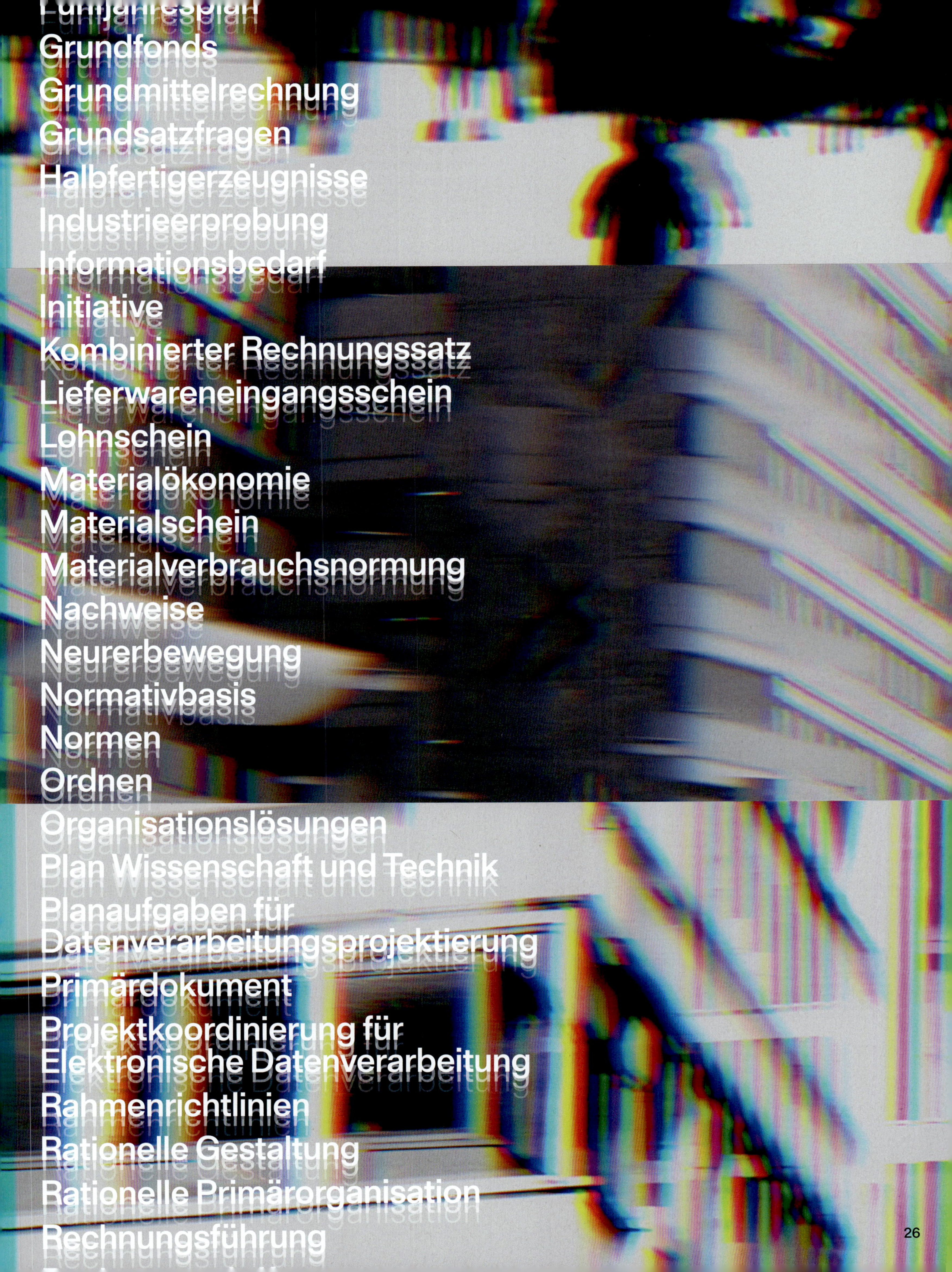

Fünfjahresplan
Grundfonds
Grundmittelrechnung
Grundsatzfragen
Halbfertigerzeugnisse
Industrieerprobung
Informationsbedarf
Initiative
Kombinierter Rechnungssatz
Lieferwareneingangsschein
Lohnschein
Materialökonomie
Materialschein
Materialverbrauchsnormung
Nachweise
Neurerbewegung
Normativbasis
Normen
Ordnen
Organisationslösungen
Plan Wissenschaft und Technik
Planaufgaben für
Datenverarbeitungsprojektierung
Primärdokument
Projektkoordinierung für
Elektronische Datenverarbeitung
Rahmenrichtlinien
Rationelle Gestaltung
Rationelle Primärorganisation
Rechnungsführung

# Karl-Heinz Adler

As early as the late 1950s, Karl-Heinz Adler (1927–2018) was experimenting with basic geometric forms and serial systems. He was interested in the spatial effects created through different arrangements. His commitment to construction-related design issues developed in the course of large-scale housing and urban development projects in the 1970s. Together with Friedrich Kracht (1925–2007) who, like Adler, was a representative of Concrete Art in the GDR, he began developing a modular system of concrete blocks in 1969. The twelve standardised elements could be combined in different ways through repetition and rotation, allowing them to be used for façades, freestanding structural walls, fountains, and other urban furniture. The concrete block system was also used on the Robotron site in Dresden, bringing computer technology into the city centre at the end of the 1960s. Adler described his artistic work as a 'philosophical view of the world', yet it was not fully recognised until after 1990, despite his membership in the GDR's Association of Visual Artists.

6 layered rectangles, tilted upwards at the centre
1984 | Collage on paper | 40×26 cm

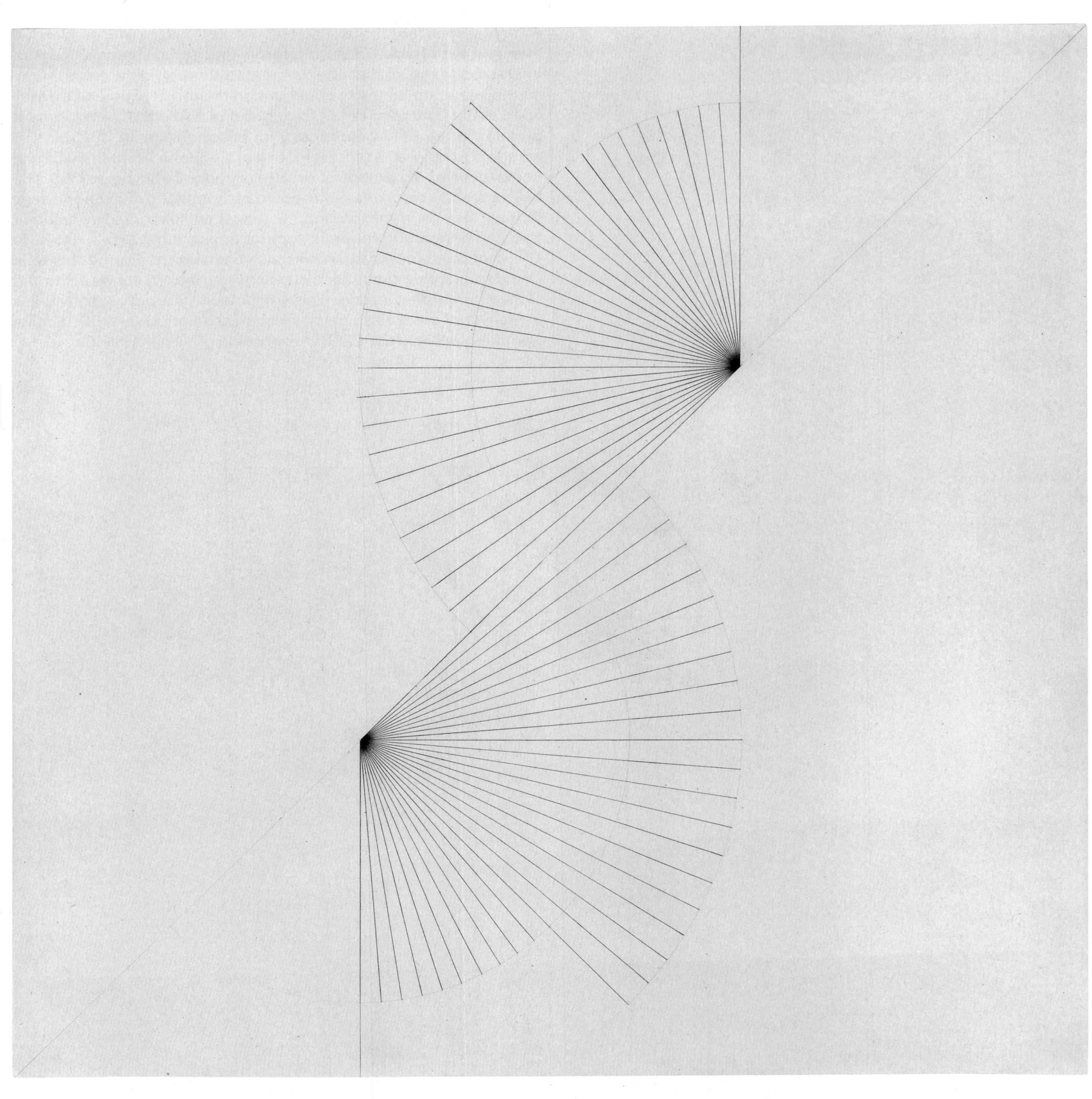

Serial lines, shifted diagonally
1968 | Graphite on cardboard | 64×64 cm

Design variant for a sculptural partition wall, Cottbus (A)
(modular system of concrete blocks)
Early 1970s | Collage on cardboard | 25×38.3 cm

Design for a light column (modular system of concrete blocks, not executed)
1977 | Collage, pen, cardboard | 38.5×35.5 cm

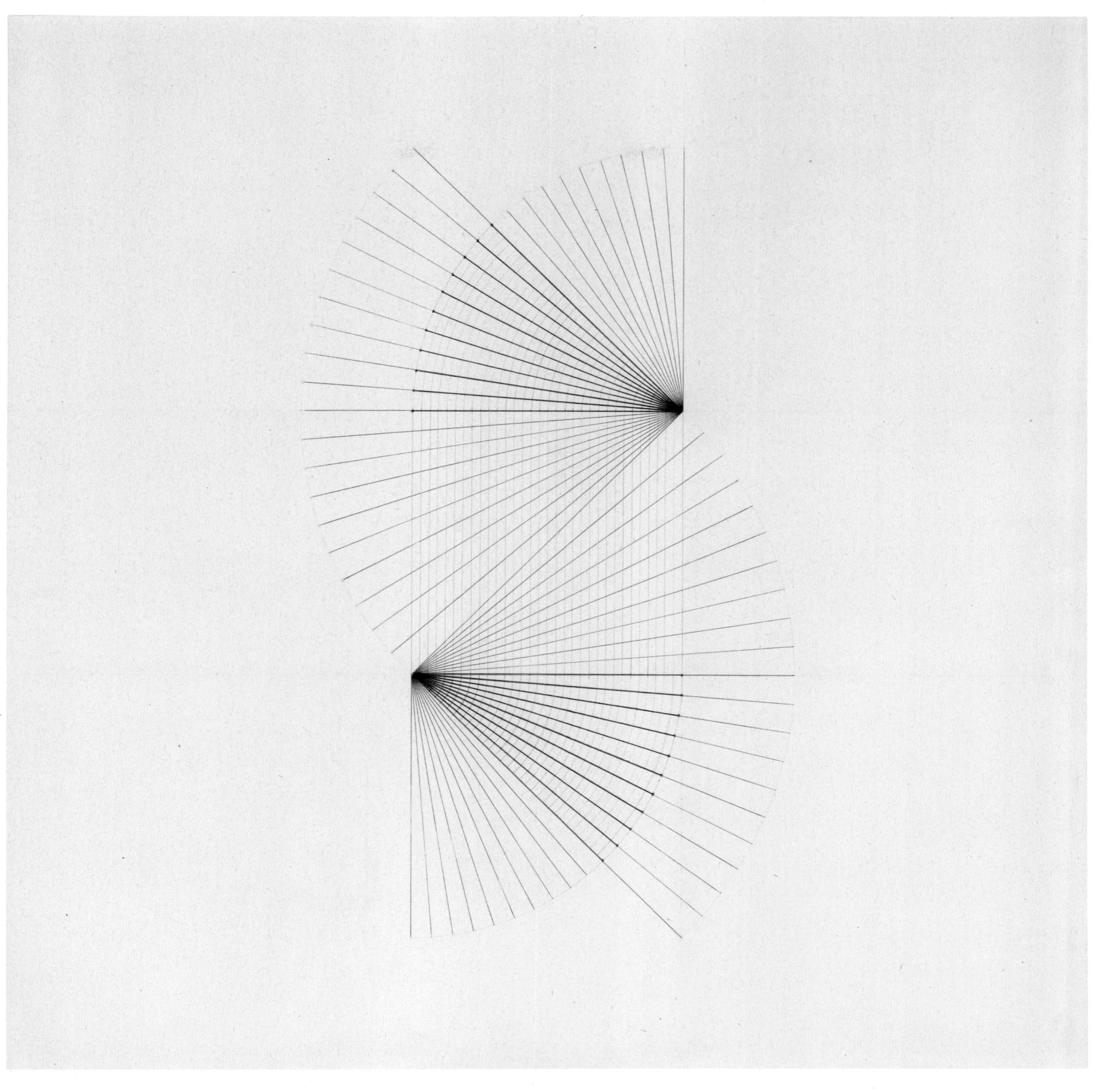

Serial lines, shifted diagonally
1968 | Graphite on cardboard | 64×64 cm

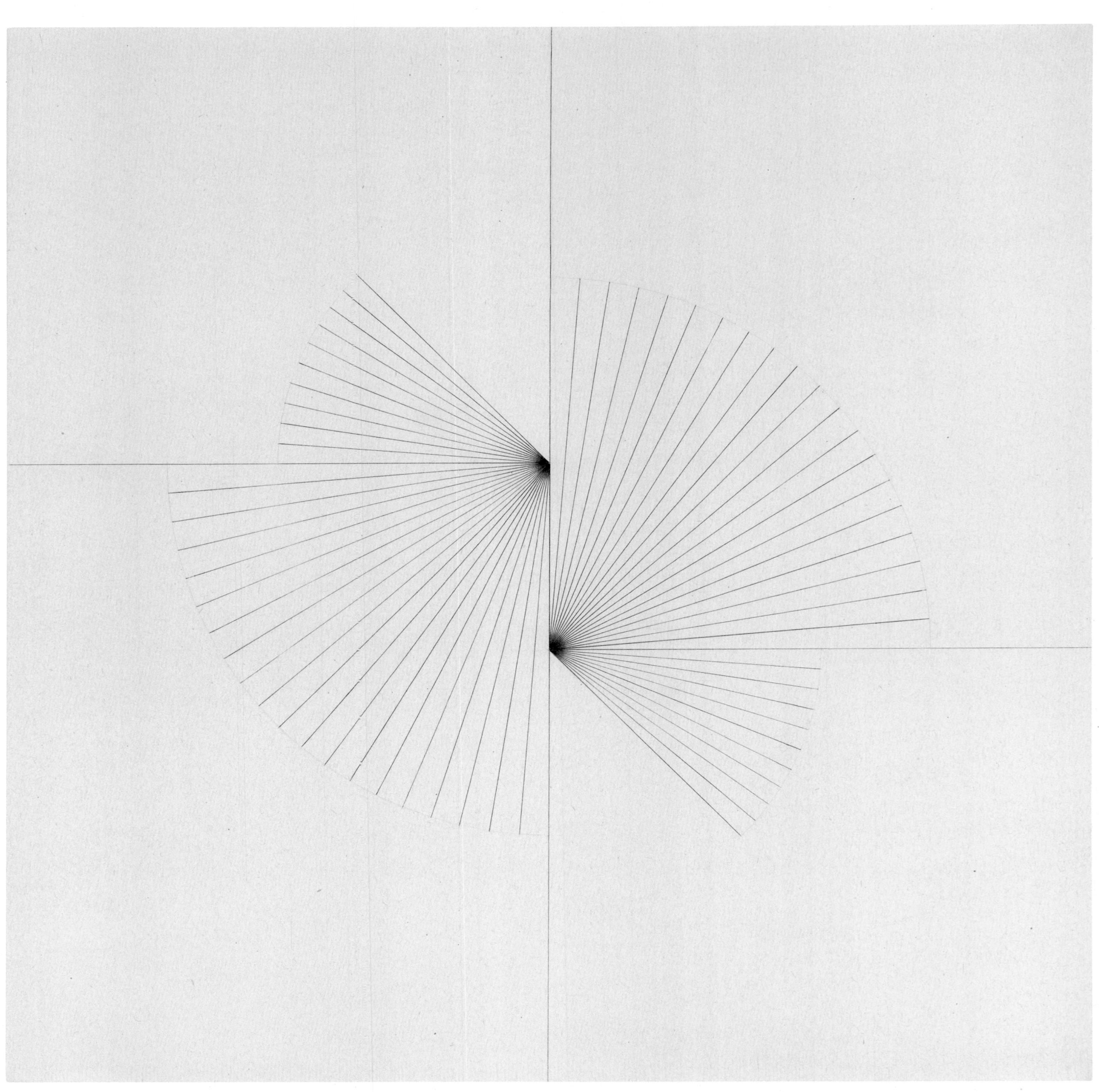

Serial lines, shifted vertically
1967/68 | Graphite on cardboard | 64×64 cm

The establishment of the state-owned combine VEB Kombinat Robotron in spring 1969 followed the GDR's policy
of consolidating production within a given industrial sector – in the case of Robotron, computers and computer
components – into a single economic unit. All enterprises
in this field across East Germany were brought together
under one combine. The economic aim was to achieve coordinated and efficient production within this new large-
scale entity, creating a planned-economy counterpart
to capitalist corporate structures.

The headquarters of VEB Kombinat Robotron were
located in Dresden. From 1969 onward, a large inner-city
complex for the combine's management and research was
built between Pirnaischer Platz and the Hygiene Museum.
Production facilities belonging to VEB Kombinat Robotron
operated at 15 sites, mostly in the south of the GDR.

The Academy of Marxist-Leninist Organisational Science
(AMLO), which opened in Berlin's Wuhlheide district in 1969,
was one of the final prestige projects of the Ulbricht era.
It was sustained by the enthusiasm for science and technology that characterised the 1960s and by Ulbricht's
interest in highly qualified socialist cadres. Conceived as
a cybernetic training centre, the AMLO was intended to
familiarise the elite from the party, the economy, and the
state administration with the methods of electronic data
processing and operations research. Through its integration of science, exhibition design, and innovative didac-
tics, the AMLO was a 'site of the future' in the GDR (Oliver
Sukrow) – perhaps its most ambitious. The week-long course
for approximately 120 participants followed a didactic
concept through which the latest findings and methods of
economic management and control were to be demonstrated
and practised – not in a lecture hall, but in a multimedia-
equipped exhibition complex. 'The elements of the exhibition
were networked according to the principle of the "cybernetic chain" – on the one hand because the devices and machines were physically connected via data and power cables,
and on the other because this corresponded, on a conceptual level, to the character of the industrial teaching
exhibition and its pedagogical goals. The climax and end-
point of the tour, programmed through four halls with
different course stations, was the architectural staging
of a working computer centre featuring a Robotron 300
behind a glass screen.' This is how art historian Oliver
Sukrow describes the exhibition circuit of the AMLO.

Only two years after its opening, the AMLO came to an
abrupt end with Ulbricht's removal from power. His successor, Erich Honecker, objected to Ulbricht's technology
offensive because it tied up too many financial resources –
resources that were henceforth to be redirected to
consumer and social programmes as part of the policy re-
orientation towards a 'Unity of Economic and Social Policy'.
By autumn 1971, the AMLO had been wound up and con-
signed to history.

# Re-organisation of Production

Systematic Heuristics was a new philosophical current
in the GDR during the 1960s. It drew on impulses from cybernetics – primarily from the field of Operations Research –
and aimed to develop a scientific methodology for problem-
solving processes in science and technology. The starting point was the work of Johannes Müller and his working
group 'Methodology of the Technical Sciences' at the
Technical University in Karl-Marx-Stadt. In 1969, Walter
Ulbricht personally championed the institutionalisation of
Systematic Heuristics within the Academy of Marxist-
Leninist Organisational Science.

Systematic Heuristics can be described as a technology of intellectual work. Rather than relying on mere
intuition, it proceeded from the assumption that compe-
tence – and ultimately the outcome of a problem-solving
process – depends significantly on the extent to which
a person commands methods and mental structures that
can be applied, albeit flexibly, across different tasks.
Its declared purpose was to make problem-solving processes conscious, to formalise them, and thus render them
more reflexive and effective. Müller followed the principle
of addressing recurring classes of problems with methods
that had proven effective in the past. These methods were
referred to as programmes and stored in a programme
library for reuse.

However, Systematic Heuristics enjoyed only a brief
heyday in the GDR. As early as 1972, the SED Politburo
under Erich Honecker resolved to dismantle the approach
institutionally, on the grounds that the class standpoint
was lacking in its approach to problem-solving. Johannes
Müller was able to continue his work only on a small scale,
under the umbrella of the Central Institute for Cybernetics, into the 1980s.

# Academy of Marxist-Leninist Organisational Science

# What Does Socialist Mean?

An alternative model of society is usually described as a utopia, a non-place. However, the imposition of a distinct time seems even more significant than the spatial rupture. Therefore, the designation *Uchronos*, non-time, would ultimately be more precise. Every revolution is also a revolt against time. It must intervene in the calendar, in the existing logic of time.

The standardisation of time at the end of the 19th century was the result of the Second Industrial Revolution. Until then, every place had its own time, determined by the course of the sun: when the sun reached its highest point in the south, it was twelve o'clock. The construction of longer railway lines in the second half of the 19th century made the introduction of a uniform standard time necessary. It was transmitted via telegraph to all railway stations along the line so that the clocks at the stations could be synchronised. Since then, a network of time zones has spanned the planet, creating a consciousness of simultaneity.

To be at the mercy of time is the stuff of tragedy. To race against it is the essence of economics.

In the early 1970s, after Erich Honecker replaced Walter Ulbricht as head of state, the GDR's new political course, which tied economic growth to social progress, brought a shift in investment priorities. In the field of electronics and electrical engineering, investment levels in 1974 reached only 68% of 1970 levels. When the first sales difficulties appeared in the mechanical engineering sector in the mid-1970s, the state leadership recognised the true significance of the 'third industrial revolution'. Microelectronics and computer technology were key industries with an impact across all sectors of the economy. At that time, productivity in microelectronics in the GDR averaged only 10 to 30% of international levels, while costs were five to ten times higher. The 'Microelectronics Plenum' convened in autumn 1976 aimed to correct this course. From then on, the GDR sought to participate in technological developments in the West, strengthen cooperation among socialist countries, and create the best possible conditions for its domestic electronics industry, in the hope of closing the technological gap.

Opinions diverge as to whether the form of society in the GDR deserved the attribute 'socialist'. The dispute often revolves around the fundamental economic question: Who decides how and what is produced, and how the produced wealth is distributed? Although the term 'people's property' (*Volkseigentum*) might suggest otherwise, workers in the factories were barely involved in economic decisions. A small group of SED party functionaries assumed the position of the ruling class in the GDR and determined all economic issues.

Already in the late 1940s, the British Trotskyist Tony Cliff had established in his book *State Capitalism in Russia* that the Stalinist Soviet Union was not a workers' state, but should rather be described as bureaucratic state capitalism, for the Soviet state acted like any capitalist entrepreneur: 'The Stalinist state is in the same position vis-à-vis the total labour time of Russian society as a factory owner vis-à-vis the labour of his employees. In other words, the division of labour is planned. But what is it that determines the actual division of the total labour time of Russian society? If Russia had not to compete with other countries, this division would be absolutely arbitrary. But as it is, Stalin's decisions are based on factors outside his control, namely the world economy, world competition. From this point of view the Russian state is in a similar position to the owners of a single capitalist enterprise competing with other enterprises.'

Tony Cliff's analysis also applied in principle to the GDR in the 1970s. While the SED had direct access to economic resources and could set its priorities, it remained ultimately dependent on the world market and its competition.

# The Violence of Time

# A. R. Penck

Just a few months after the Berlin Wall was built in 1961, A. R. Penck (1939–2017) began developing a pictorial language made up of simple figures and symbols. This was the starting point for his first *Weltbilder* (World Pictures). Penck's focus lay on the opposing political systems of East and West, and the ever-present threat of violent conflict between them. He read texts on cybernetics and turned his attention to theoretical physics and information theory. In schematic drawings such as *Computermodell* (1970), he examined the relationship between signs and information. Penck perceived society as a physical body, seeking to visualise its underlying patterns, forces, and resistances. This approach is also evident in his *20 Sketches from 1968*. His applications to study art in the GDR were unsuccessful, and he was also refused membership in the Association of Visual Artists. From the late 1960s, he came under increasing pressure from the Stasi. In August 1980, he was expatriated and moved to West Germany. Major exhibitions and teaching appointments followed.

Skizze zu Weltbild Nr. 4 (Sketch for Worldview No. 4)
1962, painted over in 1979 | Latex over ink on cardboard, mounted on canvas
75.5×95.5 cm

From the series: 20 Skizzen von 1968 (20 Sketches from 1968)
1968 | Blue ink on cardboard | 20×14.4 cm | 17.1×14.7 cm | 16.1×14.4 cm | 14.1×11.8 cm

19
A B C
A B
av. penck

22
av. penck

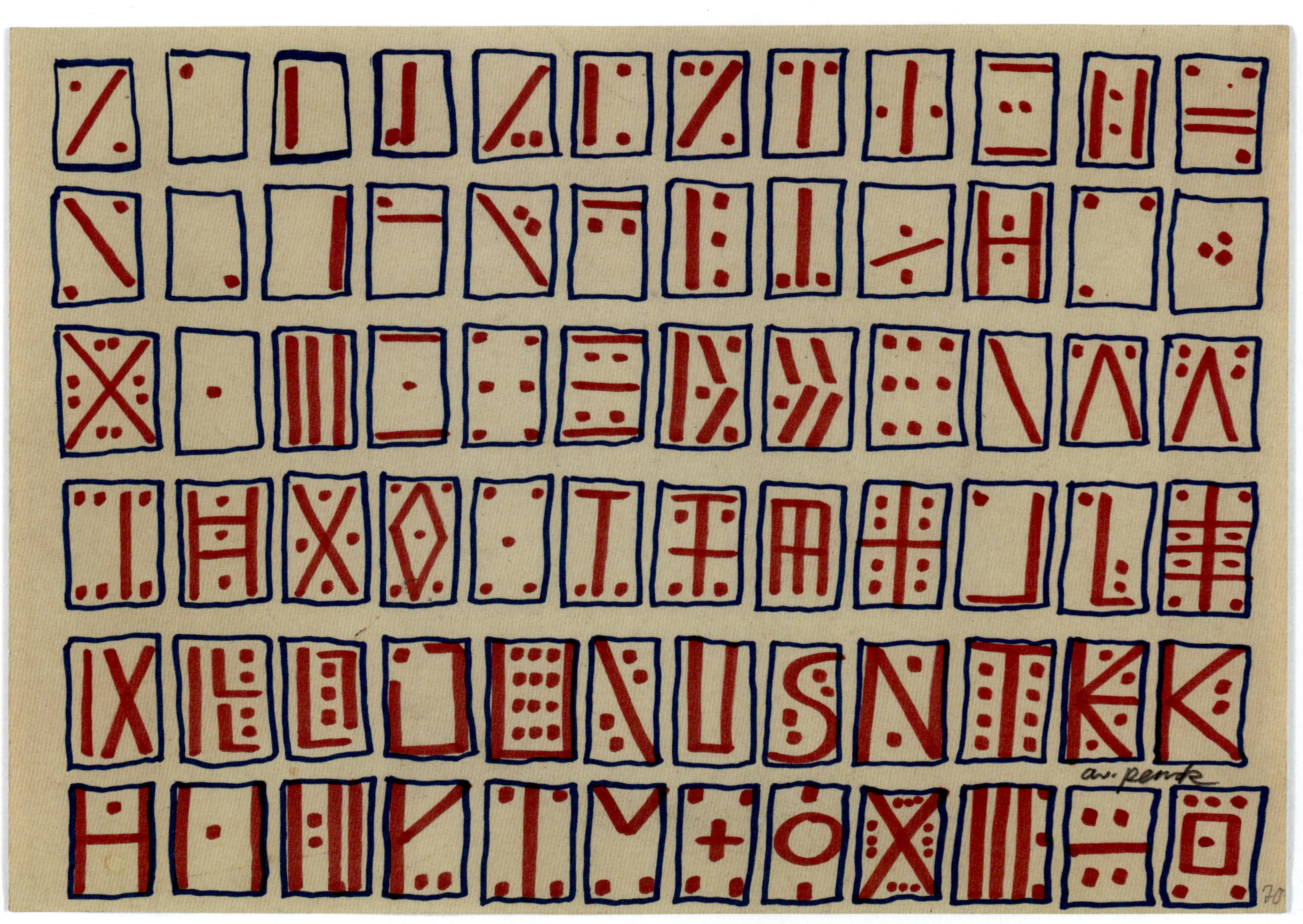

Computermodell (Computer Model)
1970 | Fiber pen | 29.8×42.2 cm

# Suzanne Treister

In her drawn diagrams, Suzanne Treister traces connections between the history of cybernetics, countercultural movements, ecology and economy, Big Tech, and state governments. The visual structure is based on alchemical illustrations from past centuries. In a new diagram, she turns to the history of cybernetics, microelectronics, and computer technology in the GDR and the USSR during the Cold War. Computing in socialist countries was developed under unique conditions shaped by central planning, limited access to Western technology, and ideological goals. Despite these constraints, these countries built innovative systems such as the Soviet ternary computer SETUN and the Elbrus supercomputers, the Robotron computers in the GDR, and Chile's visionary Cybersyn project. Revisiting socialist computing sheds light on how technology can be organised around public needs, social equity, and systemic resilience – questions that remain urgent in our current digital age.

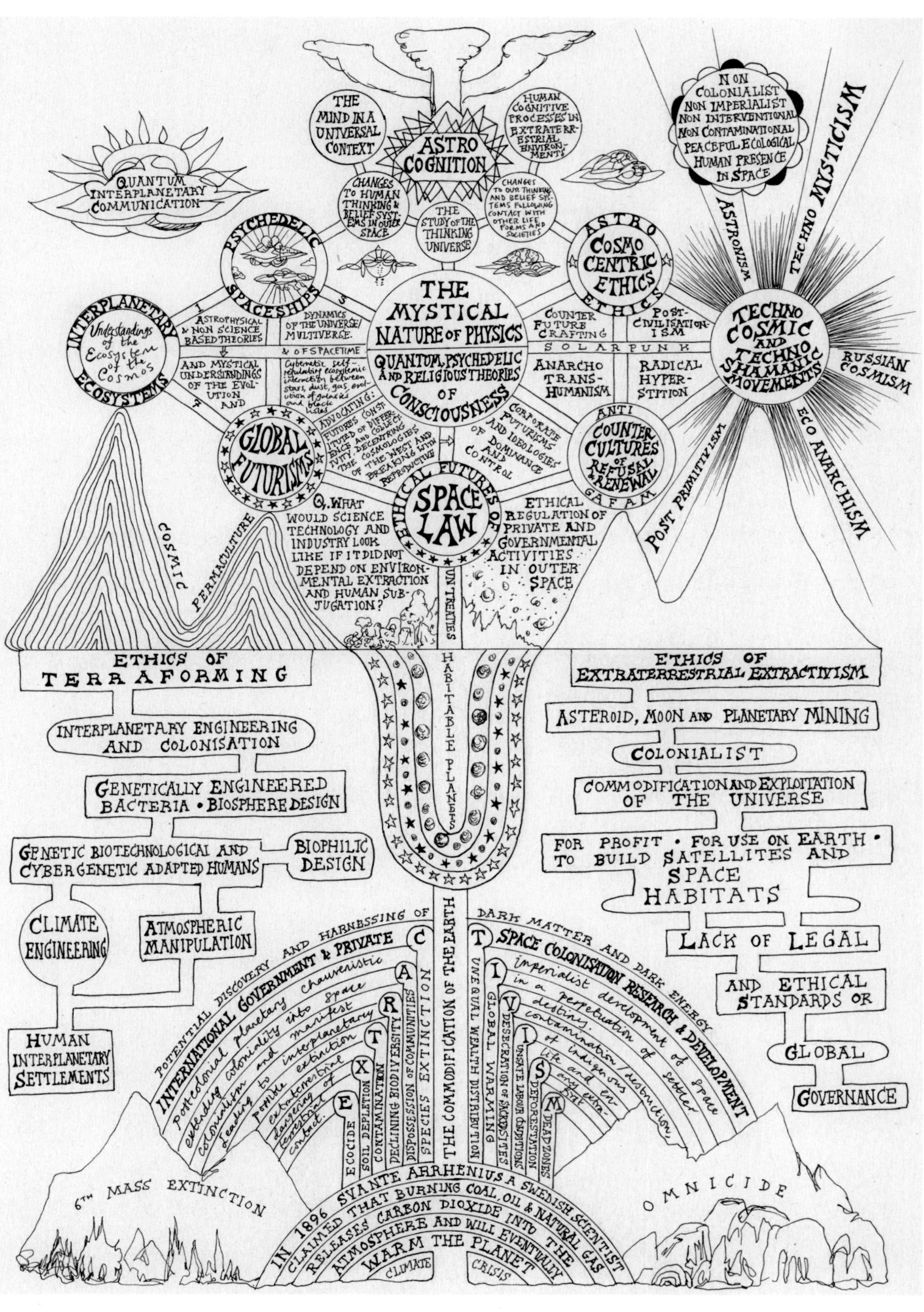

From the Potential Destruction of the Universe via Interplanetary Ecosystems and Psychedelic Spaceships to Astrocognition, from the series HEXEN 5.0 / Historical Diagrams
2023–25 | Ink on paper | Dimensions variable

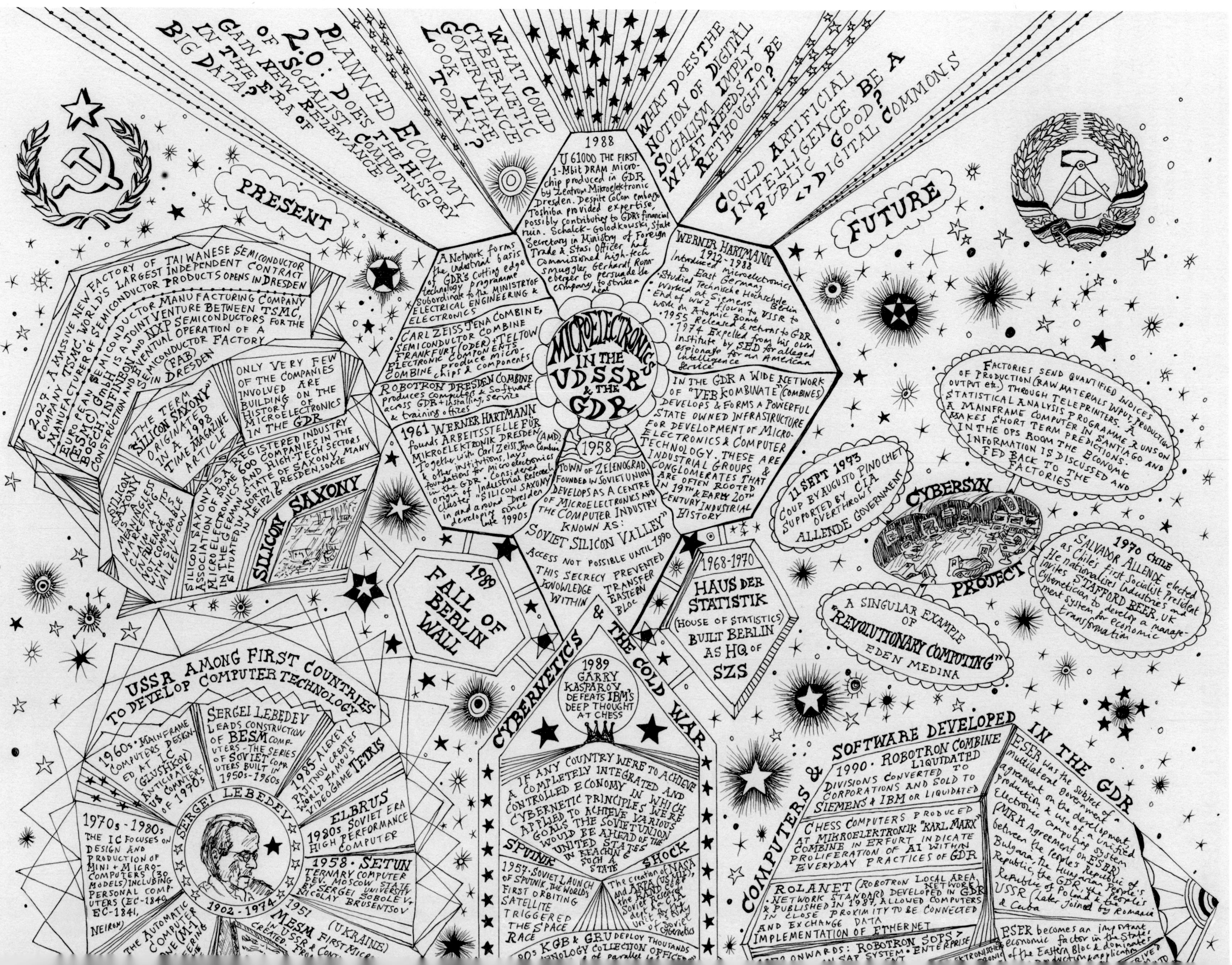

MICROELECTRONICS IN THE USSR & THE GDR
FUTURE
PRESENT
PROJECT CYBERSYN
SOFTWARE DEVELOPED IN THE GDR
COMPUTERS & THE COLD WAR
CYBERNETICS
SPUTNIK SHOCK
FALL OF BERLIN WALL
SILICON SAXONY
USSR AMONG FIRST COUNTRIES TO DEVELOP COMPUTER TECHNOLOGY
HAUS DER STATISTIK
ESER DEVELOPED IN THE GDR
COULD ARTIFICIAL INTELLIGENCE IMPLY A "DIGITAL GOOD" COMMONS?
WHAT DOES THE NOTION OF DIGITAL SOCIALISM NEED TO BE / WHAT NEEDS TO BE RETHOUGHT?
WHAT COULD CYBERNETIC GOVERNANCE LOOK LIKE TODAY?
PLANNED ECONOMY 2.0. DOES THE HISTORY OF SOCIALIST COMPUTING GAIN NEW RELEVANCE IN THE ERA OF BIG DATA?
WERNER HARTMANN
"REVOLUTIONARY COMPUTING" A singular example of — EDEN MEDINA
1970 CHILE — SALVADOR ALLENDE elected as Chile's first Socialist president
1988
1958 SOVIET SILICON VALLEY
1961 WERNER HARTMANN
1989 GARRY KASPAROV DEFEATS IBM'S DEEP THOUGHT AT CHESS
1990 ROBOTRON COMBINE LIQUIDATED
SERGEI LEBEDEV
ELBRUS
SETUN
BESM
MESM (UKRAINE)
ROLANET
KGB & GRU
1968-1970
1990
1989 FALL OF BERLIN WALL
1902-1974 SERGEI LEBEDEV

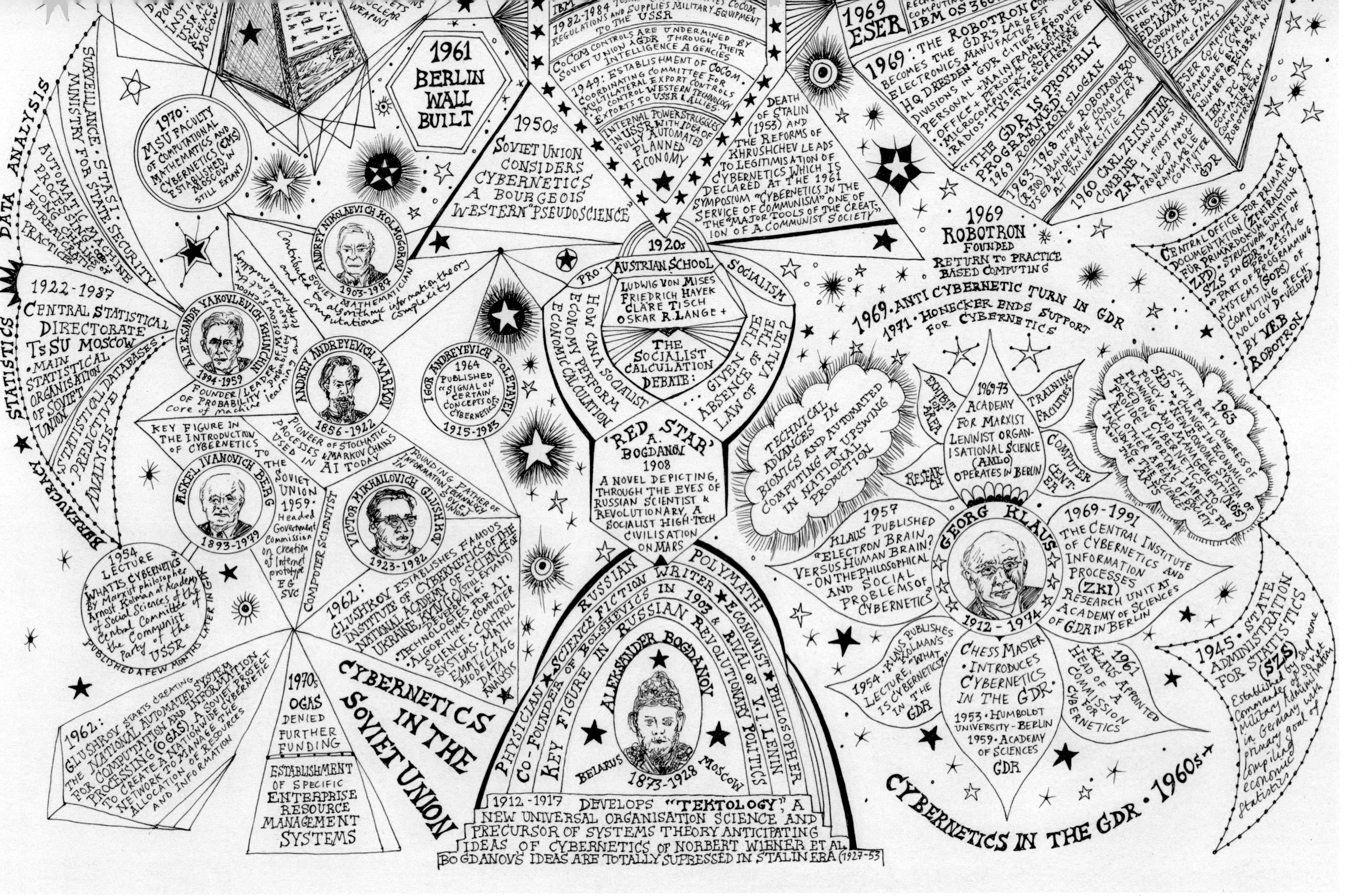

Concerning Technological Histories of Socialist Computing as Instruments for
Collective Progress, Economic Planning, Education, State Coordination and Repression
2025 | Ink on paper | Dimensions variable

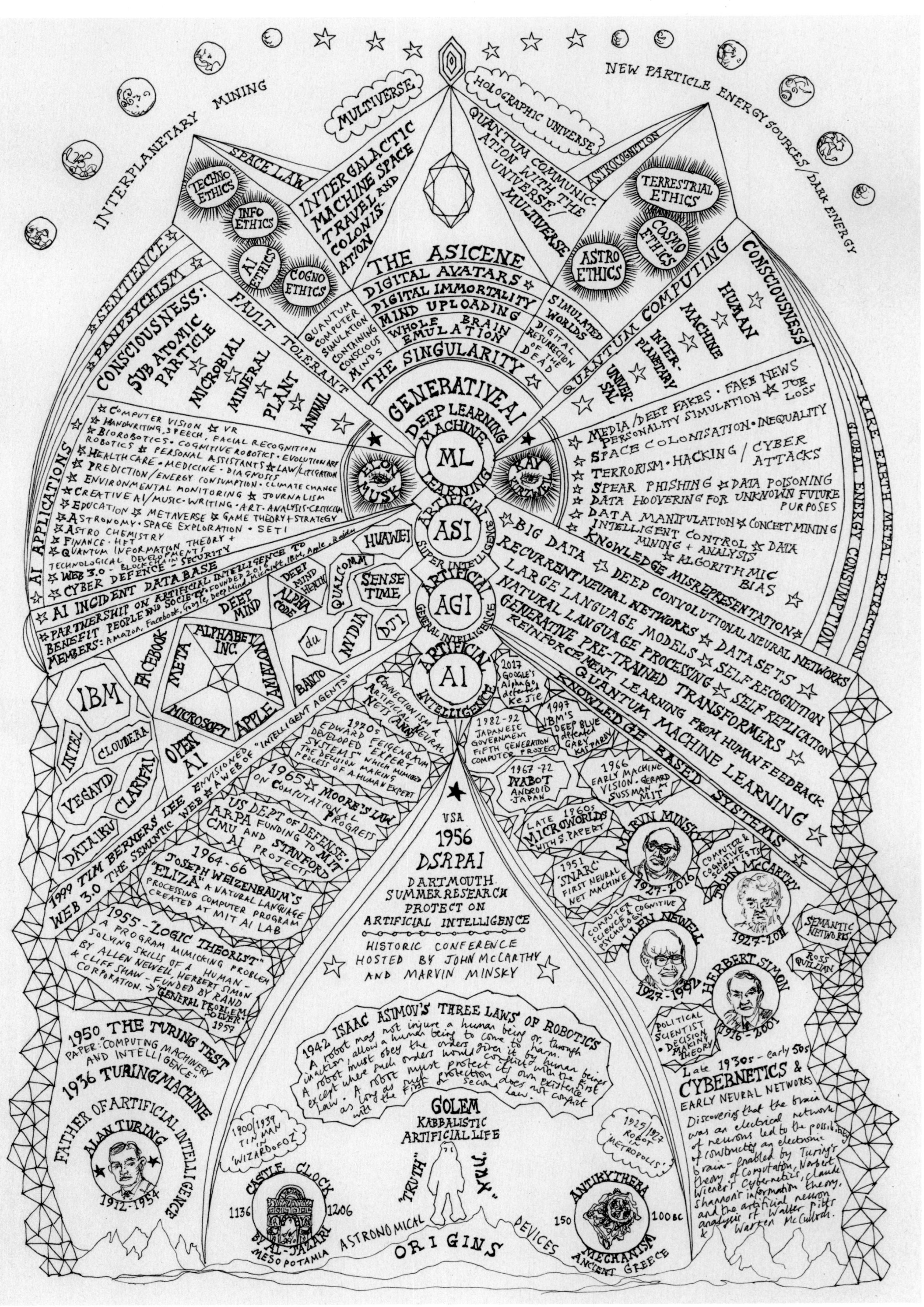


From the Golem via Deep Learning to Machine Colonisation of the Multiverse
From the series HEXEN 5.0 / Historical Diagrams
2023–25 | Ink on paper | Dimensions variable

# Against Cybernetics

With cybernetics, a new technology of domination appears in the post-war period – one that conceives of individual and social behaviours as programmed and endlessly reprogrammable. Its ideal is stability: the securing of order despite all dynamism. Its credo is adaptation: the integration of every impending disturbance. In cybernetics, it becomes apparent that the police are not merely an organ of power but also a form of thinking – a mode of thought that perpetuates a target state precisely because it stands ready for any disruption, transforming uncertainties into forecasts and intercepting the future before it can even arrive.

An enterprise, an economy, a society – everything can be represented as a circuit, calculable on the basis of data, through ever-denser information networks and the stabilising exchange between all components. And yet the circulating data converge somewhere; and yet there is a captain who makes decisions and a helmsman who executes them; a control panel and the overview it suggests; the levers and the calculability they promise.

Cybernetics transforms the world into a prison of freedom. Total transparency is its aim. It replaces the world with a simulation – a simplified, controllable replica. It dissolves every action into decision trees; it encircles life with algorithms, calculating in advance the probability of each next step. So long as cybernetics still finds itself compelled to concede that comprehensive control of human existence is not achievable, it has not yet reached its goal. But how much longer can the human being remain a source of disruption? How much longer can life resist absorption into its own simulation? And when will the door through which the future might enter finally close? Then we will be locked in a stable circuit of the present.

In the 1980s, despite the Western embargo, the GDR attempted to participate in the international division of labour in the field of microelectronics. To this end, cooperation was sought in 1986 between Kombinat Mikroelektronik Erfurt and the second-largest Japanese microelectronics group, Toshiba. The agreement was to create the conditions for the production of the 1-megabit chip in Erfurt in three stages with Toshiba's help: following improvements to the manufacturing infrastructure, the 64-kDRAM chip was to be produced with a yield of at least 60 percent functional units, and in a third stage, the 256-kDRAM chip with a yield of at least 50 percent. 'Toshiba studied the state of our technology in Erfurt, and we frequently visited Toshiba's laboratories and production facilities for consultations. Trials were run in production in Erfurt using the documentation, the results of which were in turn analysed at Toshiba. The resulting suggestions for improvement were immediately reflected in our technology,' describes Gerhardt Ronneberger, who established contact with Toshiba while at the Ministry of Foreign Trade, characterising the state of the collaboration.

The cooperation took place on the basis of a gentlemen's agreement; Toshiba had refused a formal signing of contracts for reasons of secrecy.

In June 1987, the Japanese group hit the headlines because an illegal technology transfer to the Soviet Union had become public, leading to fierce political reactions in the USA. Ten members of Congress smashed Toshiba radios on the lawn in front of the Capitol. This was a symbolic act of displacement, for the parliamentarians would have preferred to smash not just the devices, but the entire Japanese conglomerate. Toshiba strove for damage limitation and, as a result of this scandal, also terminated its cooperation with the GDR.

On 15 January 1988, a meeting took place at the Hotel Bristol between two high-ranking managers of the Toshiba group and representatives of GDR foreign trade, during which the company representatives demanded that 'all traces that could trigger even the slightest suspicion be removed'. On 9 February, in the presence of two Toshiba employees, hastily made copies – rather than the originals – of the documents on manufacturing technology for the 64- and 256-kDRAM and the mask sets for the 64-kDRAM were destroyed. In return, Toshiba undertook to immediately repay the 7.8 million dollars received to date.

The effects of this failed technology transfer were considerable. Left on its own, the GDR did not succeed in realising stable serial production of the 256-kDRAM.

# A Geopolitical Drama

# PC 1715

The Büromaschinenwerk Sömmerda, with a history dating back to 1816, had been part of Rheinmetall since 1901 and quickly developed into an important production site for typewriters and calculating machines. In 1969, the operation was initially assigned to Kombinat Zentronik, before joining Robotron in 1978. The plan was for the Sömmerda site to concentrate on printer production within the combine. Consequently, the factory's most successful product, the PC 1715, initially had to be developed 'in secret', against the resistance of the combine's centralist planning structures. The Sömmerda team benefited from first presenting their new development as a 'printer control device' at the 1983 Printer Symposium in Moscow. The Soviet side immediately recognised the value of this cost-effective workstation computer and promised to purchase at least 10,000 units. It was only this success in Moscow that opened doors within the combine for Sömmerda's in-house development. Series production began in 1985. Initially, production of 11,000 units was planned for 1986, but this figure eventually rose to 21,000: at a party conference in the factory in November 1985, the Central Committee Secretary for the Economy, Günter Mittag, abruptly imposed a 'voluntary pledge' on the workforce to produce an additional 10,000 PC 1715s. The Sömmerda team had originally intended to pledge 1,000 additional PCs in a greeting address to Erich Honecker, but Mittag increased the number tenfold in his speech. Sheer horror showed on the faces of the audience members in the front rows, yet the pledge was fulfilled the following year, and 10,000 additional PCs left the factory. Since every PC at a workstation also needed to be connected to a printer, follow-on problems arose immediately; capacity in Sömmerda was insufficient to produce additional printers alongside the additional PCs. The printers were subsequently ordered from Epson using hard currency. In other sectors, too, the supply industry faced unprecedented challenges due to the Sömmerda 'computer initiative', for while the GDR's centrally planned economy could simply order double the parts and materials to be delivered to Sömmerda, plans elsewhere were overturned, bottlenecks created, and chaos caused as a result. Nevertheless, the additional 10,000 PCs from Sömmerda changed a great deal within the GDR: computer workstations were established in numerous enterprises for the first time, meaning that the actual saving of time and effort – the rationalisation effect of IT – arrived in everyday working life in many places for the first time.

Given its restricted access to the world market, could the GDR have strived for a division of labour in the field of microelectronics within the socialist countries of Eastern Europe? Initially, the significant disparity in the economic performance of the individual countries spoke against this. In the field of microelectronics, only the Soviet Union and Czechoslovakia were potential partners. However, the GDR's relationship with the Soviet Union was ambivalent, as cooperation was geared primarily towards the needs of the Soviet economy. The GDR received hardly any microelectronic products, yet had to export a large proportion of its own manufactured goods. While a special device manufactured in the GDR contributed significantly to the creation of Soviet memory chips, no Soviet research and development results were made available to the GDR. Many fundamental questions regarding risk sharing, benefit distribution, and the binding nature of agreements remained unresolved, just as cooperation simply failed due to differing standards and norms.

# Socialist Egoisms

GDR exports in the field of microelectronics were aimed primarily at the Eastern European market. In the 1980s, approximately 70 percent of electronic components, as well as data and automation technology, went there. The GDR was able to sell its products profitably in these markets, even if they were not technologically state-of-the-art. For example, Robotron achieved profits of up to 50 percent on its exports to Eastern Europe in the late 1980s. At the same time, the West exploited the egoisms of the Eastern European states. As soon as it became known that the GDR had reached a certain technological level in microelectronics, the relevant products were removed from the CoCom list and the corresponding trade restrictions lifted. Consequently, the Eastern European states purchased the qualitatively superior and cheaper Western products. 'When it became known in the late 1980s that the GDR would soon commence serial production of fast 16-bit PC technology, the existing embargo on this point was lifted, whereupon the other Comecon countries, insofar as it was financially possible for them, preferred to fall back on the cheaper Western technology.' (Olaf Klenke)

# Sandra Schäfer

In the early 20th century, the rapid expansion of industrial production, the seemingly limitless potential for profit, and the pressing need to improve working conditions fuelled initiatives to optimise workflows. Key figures in the development of the 'scientific management' of labour were Frederick Taylor and Lillian and Frank Gilbreth in the United States and Aleksei Kapitonovich Gastev in Russia. Using photography, they studied workers' movements and created wire models for training purposes. The automation of labour advanced through powerful machinery and, from the 1970s onwards, through computer technology. However, increased productivity also led to an exponential rise in the demand for raw materials and energy. Sandra Schäfer's video work explores the relationship between humans and machines, the energy they expend, and the resources required for production. Performers recreate the movements of physical labour, while a coal plough extracts seams of coal from the rock face. The search for rare earths and new habitats sparks a struggle for dominance in outer space.

Where Gravity Fades
2025 | Video, colour, sound | 19:55 min
Room construction made of wood, wire sculptures | Dimensions variable

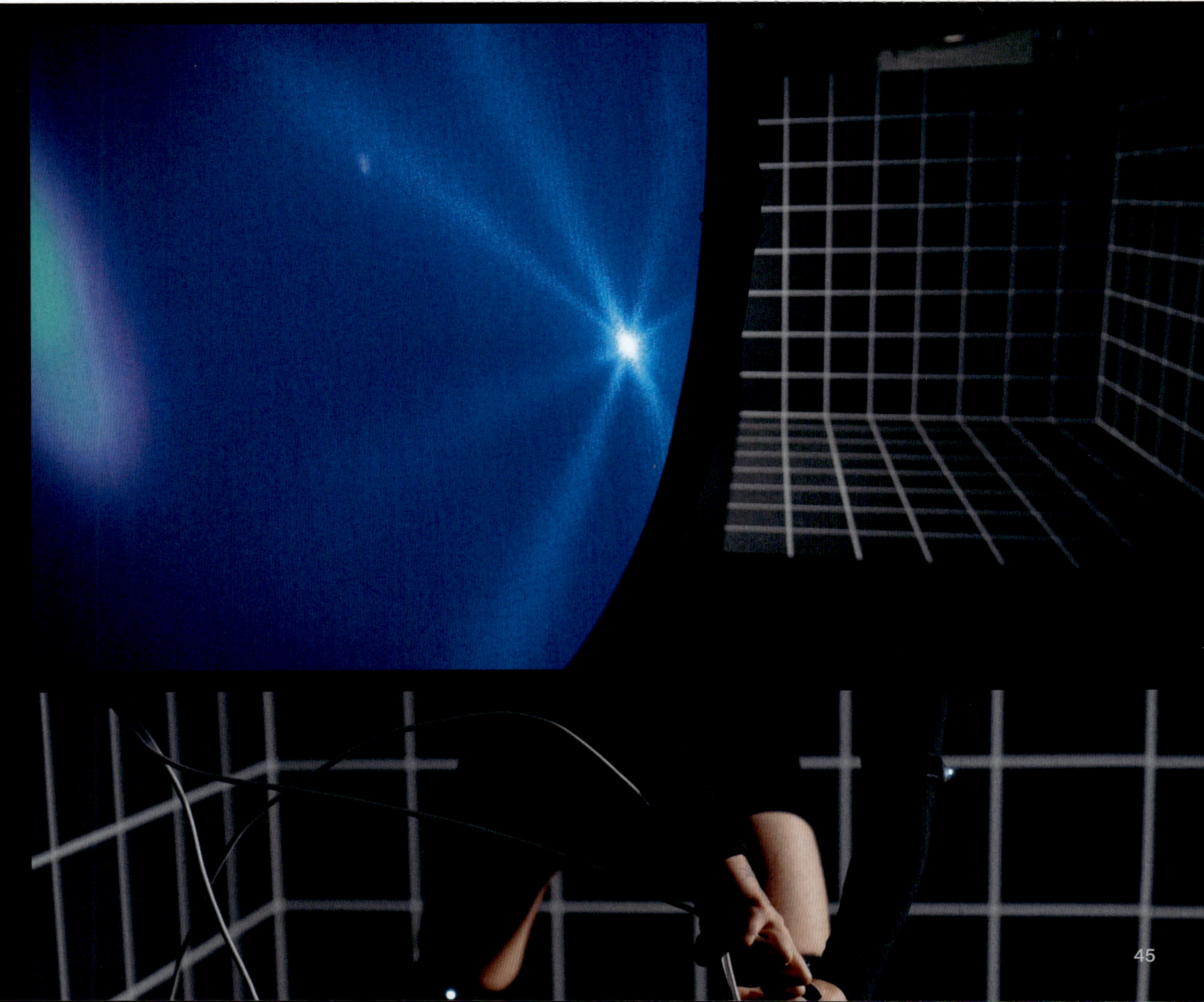

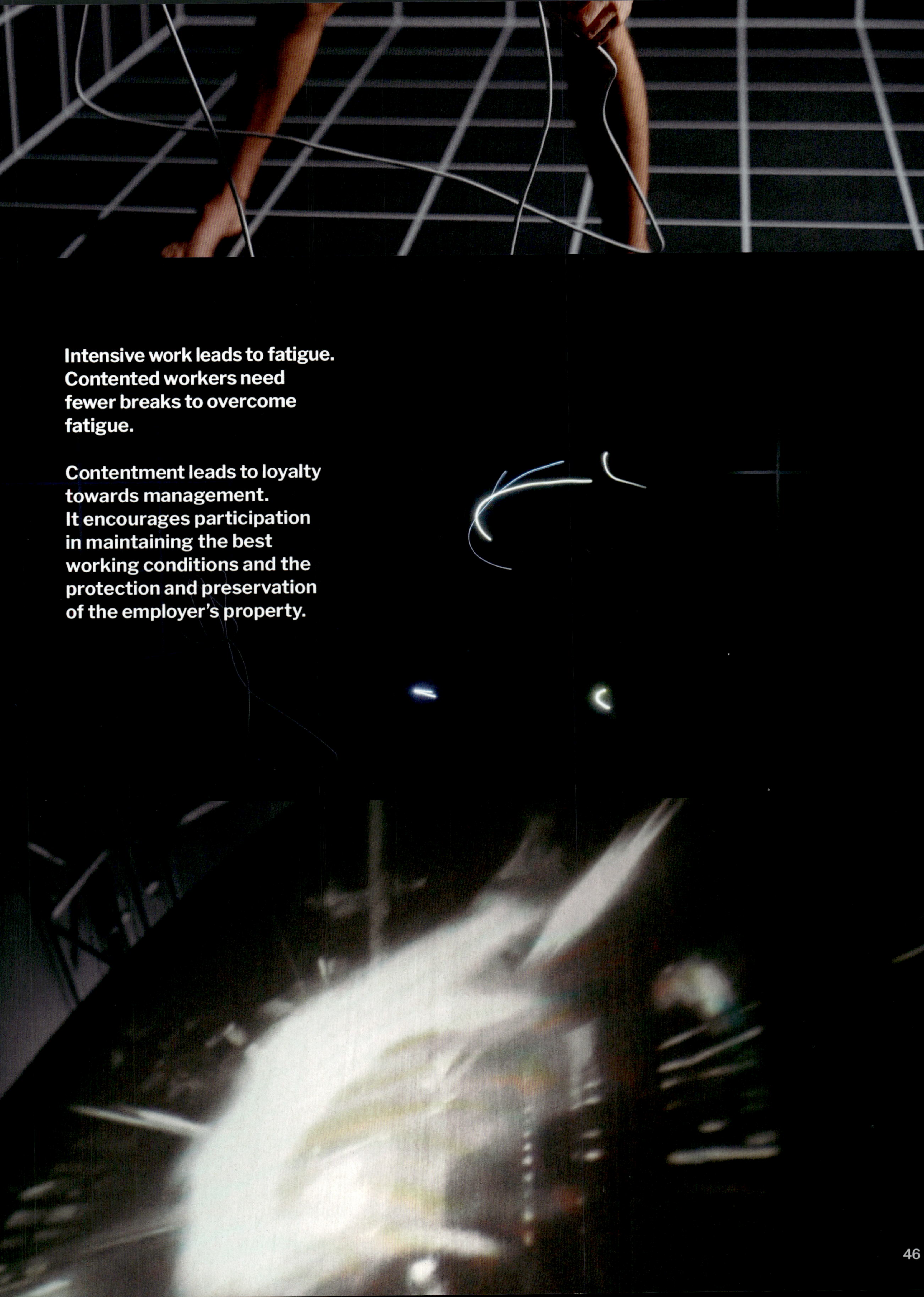

Intensive work leads to fatigue.
Contented workers need
fewer breaks to overcome
fatigue.

Contentment leads to loyalty
towards management.
It encourages participation
in maintaining the best
working conditions and the
protection and preservation
of the employer's property.

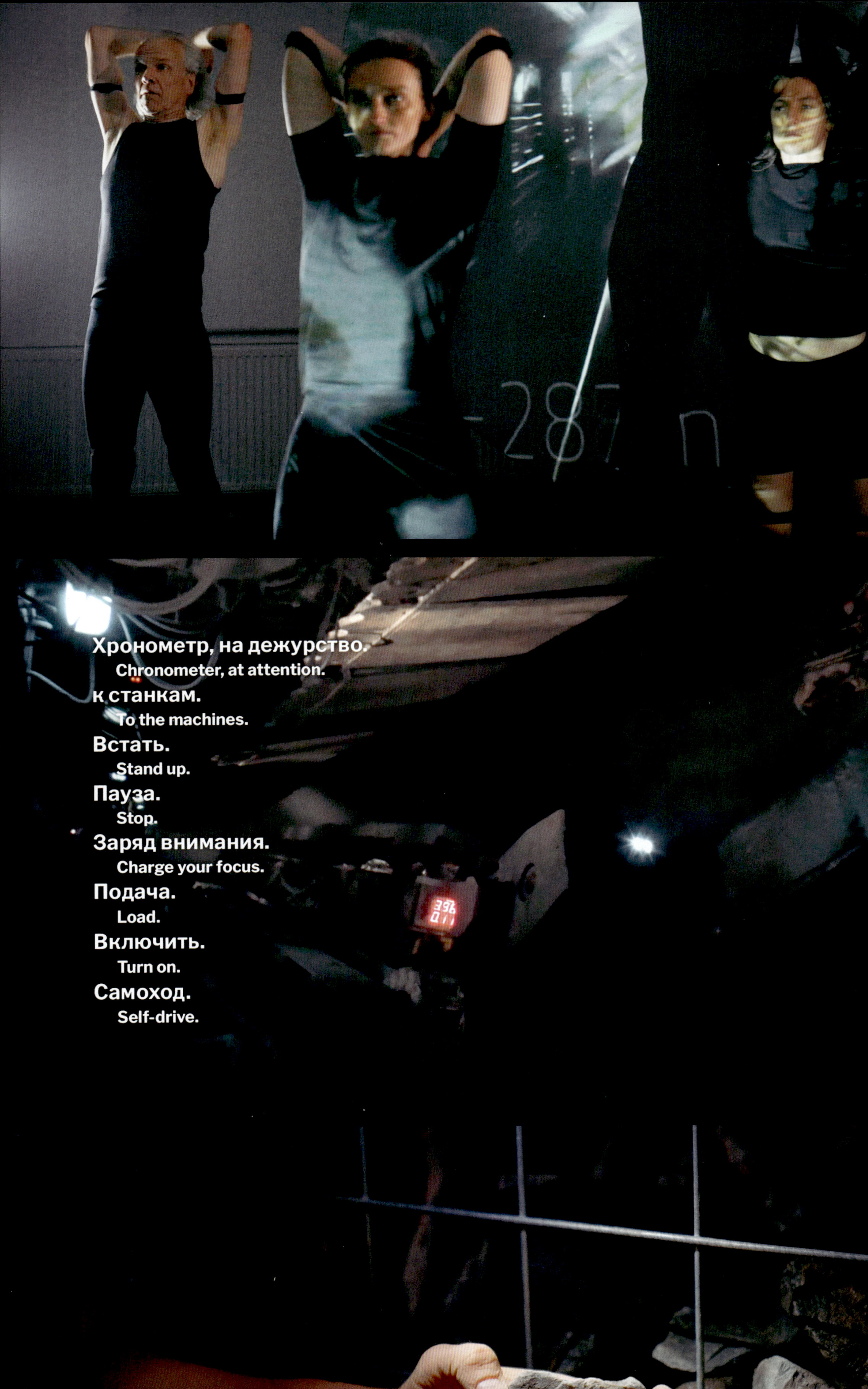
Хронометр, на дежурство.
Chronometer, at attention.
к станкам.
To the machines.
Встать.
Stand up.
Пауза.
Stop.
Заряд внимания.
Charge your focus.
Подача.
Load.
Включить.
Turn on.
Самоход.
Self-drive.

Und die Verbindung mit der Tiefe, der Wärme
And the connection with the depth, the warmth,

# Irma Markulin

Irma Markulin's motifs are based on historical photographic documents depicting the everyday working lives of female employees at the former VEB Kombinat Robotron. Markulin has perforated the anonymous portraits, recalling the punch cards once used in early data processing to store data and programmes. These cards stored information through coded patterns of holes, generated and read by electro-mechanical devices. However, the information encoded in the punch-card patterns remains unreadable to us – just like the portraits themselves, which reveal nothing about the individuals depicted. The photographs taken by Ulrich Häßler and Wolfgang Thieme for the GDR press, as well as the accompanying captions (abridged here), are held in the Federal Archives.

From the series: Biography beyond Statistics
2022 | B/w photographs, perforated | 56×56 cm

Electronics technician Antje Heilmann assembles power supplies for the new EC 1834 personal computer, 1988

Test engineer Claudia Uhlemann testing an assembly
for the EC 2655 M computer, 1985

Martina Porembski wires small components for EC 1040
computing systems, 1977

Regina Vaczo making cables for the ESER system computers,
1980

## Blueprint for Socialism: Human and Machine in the Early Soviet Union

Susanne Altmann is an art historian, author, and curator. Her research and writing focus on the history of Eastern European avant-gardes and East German art from a feminist and critical perspective.

Science and technology were intended to secure the victory of socialism over capitalism. In the early Soviet Union, political elites and progressive artists under Lenin's leadership had developed a corresponding utopian vision. How did they intend to shape society?

Today, few are familiar with the thinkers who shaped developments in Russia and the young Soviet Union between 1914 and the early 1930s – developments that later became fundamental to the structure of the GDR and the so-called Eastern Bloc. They imagined society as a living machinery that could – and had to – be organised. All aspects of life, from industry to culture, were to be modelled for maximum efficiency. In retrospect, this is often classified as a utopia, implying it was ideological and therefore unachievable. Yet at the time, the focus was very much on practical solutions. A key figure in this regard was Alexander Bogdanov with his organisational-scientific approach, 'Tectology', a precursor to systems theory. This scheme allowed processes like industrialisation or literacy campaigns to be broken down into clear planning units. The concept of tectology most prominently represented the idea of structuring and linking all areas of the new state and economic system. Art and culture played a central role, as evidenced by the implementation of the 'Proletkult' programme. Nationwide, culture was to be made accessible to the working class – then largely still a massive peasantry – through formats such as creative circles, theatre, literature, and film, along with education and a sense of identification with Soviet ideals. It was a highly modern network model comprising of many nodes, naturally under central control. This systematic approach was also evident in the industrialisation of that vast country. Lenin's formula 'Communism is Soviet power plus electrification' could be understood through such a super-structure. The new infrastructures did not appear overnight but emerged gradually – manifested as administrative units and driven by a forced techno-optimism. For example, in the 1920s, Aleksei Kapitonovich Gastev developed concepts for the rationalisation of human labour based on mechanical principles. Using then-new media such as film and photography, he analysed and visualised individual work processes; here, we encounter the communist interpretation of US-imported Taylorism.

Interestingly, Gastev was also a lyricist. He wrote poems about the 'poetry of the worker's blow'. Just as with Bogdanov, who wrote utopian novels, art was naturally integrated into this new way of thinking. Gastev viewed the emergence of a new human in socialist society as a *Gesamtkunstwerk* [total work of art]. The new human of the future was intended to 'combine the agility of animals with the precision of a machine'.

But it soon became apparent that humans were not quite as machine-like as envisioned. Furthermore, the creative avant-garde was silenced soon after the consolidation of power by Stalin, who became General Secretary of the Central Committee of the Communist Party in 1922. And yet, the developments of this brief period echoed for a long time, for example in the later enthusiasm for cybernetics and cosmonautics. The visions for this new world were produced in think tanks like the Vkhutemas, the 'Higher Art and Technical Studios' in Moscow. Before Stalin dissolved the Vkhutemas in 1930, the architecture and urban planning departments had already devised 'flying cities' with vertical and horizontal transport systems. There, the architect and artist El Lissitzky designed modernist, minimalist living cells that still feel relevant today. Progress in the communist sense was increasingly reflected in utilitarian design. After phases of Cubo-Futurism and Suprematism, artists such as Lyubov Popova, Varvara Stepanova, El Lissitzky, and Alexander Rodchenko turned radically away from painting as a representational art. In the movement known as Productivism, they recast themselves as engineers of progress. They found a non-elitist, socially relevant purpose in the design and manufacture of everyday objects such as clothing, textiles, furniture, tableware, propaganda posters, and even stage sets.

How relevant was the utopian era of the young Soviet Republic to developments in the GDR?

The phenomena described earlier, with their industrial-romantic and idealistic character, could not, of course, be transferred seamlessly to the second half of the century or to the newly planned communist countries. In between lay the Stalinist hardening of ideology. Moreover, many of the experiments had already failed in practice. And yet, the 'actually existing' socialism they aspired to was still rooted in these utopian origins. The expectations placed on the future socialist world order and value system were correspondingly untenable. From today's perspective, it almost seems as if the Soviet officials, fuelled by a residual idealism from 1917 and the outcome of the war, saw the possibility of starting over again with all the attendant aspects – industrialisation, economic planning, the development of the new human, building and reconstruction, and so on. It was a restart intended to confirm the validity of the communist worldview at the beginning of the Cold War and during the intensification of a binary world logic.

An important aspect of the Soviet avant-garde, which you also illuminate in your book *When Technology Was Female* (2024), was gender equality. While still an integral part of this early tech utopia, in the GDR it was reduced to merely deploying women in production.

Soviet ideology designed the image of a new human formed independently of gender. This figure was viewed as a machine to be optimised. When Gastev used sketches and diagrams to show the stages in which a hammer was to be lifted and brought down, it did not matter whether the person executing the task was a woman or a man. Interestingly, in the GDR, the failure of this utopian doctrine can be traced in the images of exhausted female workers that appeared increasingly in art. The typology of femininity often reveals how techno-optimism, working-class heroism, the focus on proletarian production, and Marxist materialism falter. In 1970s East Germany, images of women began to appear, initially in painting, that addressed pessimism, melancholy, and isolation in connection with professional life. In artistic photography, this emerged even earlier, for instance in images of women in industrial plants. In these images, we see the idea of automation in the service of humanity fall to pieces before our very eyes.

## Software for the Planned Economy

Francis Hunger is an artist and media scholar. His research focuses on the history of data processing in socialist countries, especially on software development at Robotron.

**Your work takes bureaucratic practices as its starting point, rather than cybernetics, which is discussed far more frequently. Why is that?**

In contemporary art and media theory, cybernetics is often employed as a catch-all term to frame the history of technology. However, cybernetics is an academic programme that developed from the 1950s onwards and was heavily influenced by the United States. It did resonate strongly among academics internationally in the 1960s and 1970s, but I propose a different focus: namely on the non-academic, pragmatic development and application of computing technology and office machines. These were simply tools that enabled cooperation – they were not born out of cybernetic considerations. They evolved from previous information practices, such as double-entry bookkeeping or the use of spreadsheets. With the onset of industrialisation, knowledge needed to be organised and automated to a greater degree. The complexity of organisational processes in production – and indeed, in society as a whole – cannot be grasped solely as cybernetic control processes. Historically speaking, bureaucracy and statistics – that is, techniques of sorting, addressing, and ordering – are more significant.

**A centre for the production of office machines had developed in Saxony and Thuringia even before the Second World War. How did the transition to the Third Industrial Revolution take shape there?**

Electronic computing technology in post-war East Germany developed out of advanced technology research. In the 1950s, the first GDR mainframe computer, named Oprema [Optik-Rechen-Maschine, or Optics Calculation Machine], was manufactured at Carl Zeiss Jena, followed by the ZRA 1. It was used to calculate optical lenses and curvatures, a task previously performed by humans. These calculations had been broken down into individual steps, as is known from Taylorism. In the end, the partial results were assembled. Computers then replaced this calculation work. The mechanisation of mental labour was the entry point into the Third Industrial Revolution.

**The collection of statistical data plays an important role for the socialist planned economy and the development of computing technology in general.**

The historical prerequisites for the planned economy were the plan itself and the recording of production capacities. The Haus der Statistik on Alexanderplatz in Berlin was built in the late 1960s as the headquarters of the GDR's Central Administration for Statistics. This was also home to what was known as the Central Office for Primary Documentation, established to standardise the manufacturing documents used in factories to coordinate production workflows. It had been created by law; the standardisation of manufacturing records was so important that it was treated as a matter of state. The functionaries launched a research programme for this purpose; they went into the factories and spoke with dispatchers and others to prepare this standardisation for electronic data processing.

**In the USSR, work was already underway in the 1960s on a nationwide networked, automated system for data processing. It was called 'OGAS'. Was there any consideration of implementing it in the GDR?**

The planned economy in the GDR had, of course, been introduced according to the Soviet model – a Prussian interpretation of it, if you will. A large part of the state leadership had returned from exile in the Soviet Union. They attempted to establish the planned economy in an optimised form. The idea of a planned economy networked via computers played a central role in this. However, OGAS did not prevail in the USSR; instead, it was undermined out of fear of too much transparency. Benjamin Peters describes this in detail in his book *How Not to Network a Nation: The Uneasy History of the Soviet Internet.* In the GDR, Robotron began to work on similar ideas for application in factories with the modular software SOPS.

**Under the ESER agreement (Unified System of Electronic Computing), which was concluded in 1969, Robotron's founding year, various socialist countries were intended to cooperate closely.**

In the GDR, it had already been recognised in the mid-1960s that they could not keep up with international standards in the field of computing technology on their own. We are talking about room-filling mainframes here. The initial attempt to achieve a bilateral agreement with the USSR failed. For political reasons, the USSR wanted a multilateral agreement with the various socialist countries. Alongside the GDR and the USSR, the People's Republics of Bulgaria, Hungary, and Poland were involved; the People's Republic of Romania and Cuba joined later. This multilateral government commission then agreed on the Western IBM 360 system as the uniform ESER standard. ESER technology was deployed in factories in the participating countries and presented at trade fairs, including in Leipzig.

**So, IBM software was used on socialist computers?**

The idea was to potentially run Western software from IBM on Eastern Bloc computers, too. In part, this succeeded, but adaptations were necessary. Some of the adaptations were made directly, and where that was not possible, the GDR engineers drew inspiration and produced their own versions – a procedure quite common in software programming in both East and West at the time.

**Despite the cooperation efforts, the relationship between the USSR and the new socialist countries remained an imperial one. There was little flow of information from the USSR into these countries. Raw materials, technology, and know-how did make their way from the GDR to the USSR, but barely the other way around.**

In the interviews I conducted with former Robotron staff, complaints were voiced that they could not access knowledge held in the USSR. Robotron then developed its own software systems such as BASTEI, an early database software, or the modular system SOPS. Prior to that, work had focused on bespoke solutions for the chemical industry, rail vehicle manufacturing, food production, and more. However, because one chemical plant operated completely differently from the next, and the software was not transferable between factories, the idea emerged in the 1970s to build a system with compatible modules – covering material logistics, workforce administration, payroll accounting, distribution, and so forth. SOPS was deployed in many factories. With its introduction, these plants were reorganised to ensure production conformed to a computational logic in the first place. The earlier step of standardised primary documentation was a crucial prerequisite for this.

**Was the SOPS system a success?**

SOPS ran on all ESER-compatible computers, which were exported as far as Cuba. Many countries adopted the system because it could be adapted to very different factories. Incidentally, I consider Robotron's SOPS to be more relevant than the Cybersyn project from Chile, which has received a lot of attention in recent discussions about the socialist planned economy, as well as in the arts. Eden Medina wrote the brilliant book *Cybernetic Revolutionaries: Technology and Politics in Allende's Chile* on the subject. Cybersyn always remained a dream; it never functioned effectively, if only because it existed for such a short time. SOPS, on the other hand, was used for socialist economic planning for over 20 years. Of course, the story of this Robotron software does not lend itself to such a dazzling narrative. Cybersyn did, after all, have the control room magnificently designed by Gui Bonsiepe, which conjures a very memorable image. But in terms of the organisation of the economy, SOPS was much more effective.

## The Path to the 1-Megabit Chip

As an engineer and scientist at the Centre for Microelectronics Dresden (ZMD), Jens Knobloch made significant contributions to East Germany's microelectronics industry and research sectors. In the 1990s, he campaigned for the industry's survival in Dresden. Among other roles, he was the Chief Designer for the development of the U 61000 1-megabit chip.

**We are discussing East German microchip development, specifically how information was obtained through illegal trade that circumvented embargoes. You worked at the Centre for Microelectronics Dresden (ZMD); what were your duties there?**

I joined the ZMD in 1973 and headed the development department. It was later incorporated into the Fraunhofer Institute, where I continued to work after 1990. From the mid-1980s, I was responsible for the development of the 1-megabit chip. Prior to that, I had already been involved in the development of the 64-kilobit chip, which was required for Robotron computing technology. Then came the 256-kilobit chip. These steps were the international standard; a new memory generation was added roughly every three years. After the 1-megabit chip, the 4-megabit chip would have been next.

**The files of the Stasi [the GDR state security service] contain a great deal of information on how data was purchased from Toshiba for the 1-megabit chip project. Why was this information needed?**

Our own research and development work for the 1-megabit chip was already underway at that time. However, the Stasi wanted to install a 'double floor' – a safety net – in case something went wrong. I wasn't even aware of this initially. As Chief Developer, it was naturally clear to me that the Stasi was watching us, but I only learned of these specific activities during the actual development work on the 1-megabit chip. I was questioned about the status of development and what items needed to be procured.

We had almost finished our own design when the Toshiba information was presented to me – under the highest level of secrecy. However, it didn't yield much for our development. It is important to know that two lines of development existed in GDR microelectronics: the VEB Kombinat Mikroelektronik in Erfurt, and the VEB Kombinat Carl Zeiss Jena with the ZMD in Dresden. There was definitely a rivalry between them. The Directors General – Heinz Wedler in Erfurt and Wolfgang Biermann in Jena – did not trust each other an inch. Wedler was convinced that we wouldn't manage it in Dresden anyway, and hoped for success via the information procured by the Stasi. Biermann, on the other hand, relied on our in-house design. His goal was to make the equipment produced in Jena suitable for the world market. For that, he needed his own 1-megabit chip to demonstrate what the equipment could do. Furthermore, the 1-megabit chip was naturally important as a component for the new generation of Robotron computers.

**In the Stasi documents, there is repeated mention of a mask set and documentation, or a 'script', regarding the microchips. What does this refer to?**

Producing the chip in the clean room involved over 400 individual steps. Every step was noted in the script; for example, how long and at what temperature the wafer (semiconductor material) must be annealed, or the concentration of etchant applied to it. All parameters must be documented. That is the content of the script. However, such a script presupposes that the exact same equipment is available. But the principle in Jena was to achieve the best results using their own equipment. Therefore, we couldn't do much with the scripts copied from Toshiba other than look at them, which was, of course, somewhat useful. But we simply didn't have certain equipment, such as the laser testers used to repair defective circuits. We had to repair them using complicated workarounds.

When I explained to the procurement team that we couldn't do much with the information for these reasons, they felt slighted, as they had procured the information at great risk. The same applied to the masks. The end product of the design process was a mask set – structured masks that are placed on the silicon during exposure. But these can only be used in close coordination with the script. This made the mask set worthless for our script and our technology.

What I only learned after the unification of Germany was that in Erfurt, where no development work was done, the team simply tried out the Toshiba mask set with their own script. The result was naturally useless. It is quite similar to porcelain. Here in Saxony, we didn't have the same kaolin used to make porcelain in China. So they looked at what was available in the Ore Mountains, and that is how Meissen porcelain came to be – made in a different way and with different materials, but the result was comparable. The 1-megabit chip had to be completely identical to those on the world market. We simply manufactured it differently from Toshiba.

**But you did have the Toshiba script in your hands?**

Yes. It was a so-called 'Confidential Classified Matter'. Only a few people were allowed to see such documents at all; I was one of them. I had a sealed steel cabinet in my office, and I also had to lock the office itself with a seal in the evening. Even so, I wasn't allowed to take the script with me. I had to go to a special, bug-proof room. I sat there at a table with the two people who had procured it. I leafed through it for half an hour and said: 'This is of no use to us at our current stage of development.' Our first mask designs were already on the way to realisation.

**The Stasi files contain information that the Toshiba managers became uneasy after the Toshiba scandal was exposed, and demanded that the Stasi destroy all information handed over to it. A Toshiba delegation then came to Erfurt to witness the destruction, which was carried out chemically and mechanically. However – according to the files – copies were made, which were then destroyed instead of the original masks.**

I also only learned about the destruction operation after the Wall fell. It is commonly assumed there was only one GDR, one planned economy, and one line of development. But that wasn't the case. There were fierce rivalries. These were also battles for spheres of influence within the Central Committee (ZK) of the SED. That is why I knew nothing of the attempts in Erfurt for a long time. However, we were certain that our path would lead to success regardless. The Stasi always believed we couldn't do it. There was a lot of self-doubt at play. In the end, we managed it after all.

**Commissioned Photography in the VEB Halbleiterwerk Frankfurt (Oder)**

Rita Große was one of the few self-employed photographers in the GDR. From 1974 to 2005, she ran a photography studio in Leipzig. She specialised in industrial photography, particularly for plants and conglomerates such as the VEB Halbleiterwerk (state-owned conglomerate for semi-conductors) in Frankfurt (Oder).

**After training as a photo laboratory technician, you completed a Master in photography in 1969. How did you become a self-employed industrial photographer?**

I first undertook my apprenticeship in Leipzig at the PGH-Fotostudio with Johanna Zeißig – who unfortunately is no longer so well-known today. With her, I began by learning the various techniques for lighting different materials such as wood, glass, and metal. Additionally, I assisted her on assignments. Then I worked as a photographer in state-owned industrial conglomerates, where we applied a special photographic film technique that was developed in the GDR to duplicate technical drawings. Although in the GDR, being self-employed was only indirectly possible, after undertaking my Master degree, I managed to build up a small company of my own. Bit by bit, I obtained the necessary technology while continuing to take on commissions for the duplication of technical drawings. Through this, the opportunity soon arose to photograph industrial plants.

**You took photographs for various state-owned conglomerates, for example the VEB Kombinat Holz und Kulturwaren (wood and cultural goods combine) and the VEB Kombinat Fortschritt Landmaschinen ('progress' agricultural machinery combine). The plant for semi-conductors in Frankfurt (Oder) was GDR's biggest producer of microelectronic components and chips and exported to many other socialist countries. How did this assignment come about?**

In order to take photographs there, a specific technical set-up was required that only a few photographers in the GDR had access to. Because the photographic film was not particularly light-sensitive, it was necessary to synchronise multiple flash devices in order to light up the big industrial halls. My husband was an electrician, and he built a custom-made set-up for me so that I could take photos in the plants – which meant that I had a competitive advantage. Additionally, in the case of the semi-conductor plant, the assignment arose not through the usual channels, but rather via a personal contact: a friend of my husband. It was something of a sensitive matter to work there as a photographer. This meant that trust was very important. From 1980 to 1988, I would work there several times a year.

**Were there things in the plant that you were not allowed to photograph?**

Yes. The technology from the West, which probably found its way into the factory via Stasi espionage. How exactly, I never found out. If something was supposed to be covered up, they would get a few people with drawings to pose in front of it, for example. And voila, you wouldn't see a thing. For this reason, other photographers or the press were only allowed to photograph in certain areas, or on special occasions, for which necessary preparations were made.

**What did you photograph in the plant?**

I would photograph products, for example the microchips produced there, as well as processes relating to workflow and production. The photos were used for company brochures and flyers that were taken to the spring and autumn trade fairs in Leipzig. The work in the plant was very demanding, and it required a great deal of precision. In the production halls, countless women sat in front of microscopes, inspecting the silicon discs. Many of them came from Poland and crossed the border every day to work at the plant. There was a contract between the GDR and the People's Republic of Poland in order to meet the high demand for labour. The Polish workers were greatly appreciated at the plant. Many of them spoke German. In order to photograph the clean rooms in which the microchips were produced, we had to thoroughly clean all the equipment, from cables to camera. To enter, we had to wear white suits and pass through several light traps. I was also able to photograph the silicon ovens – the silicon's blue halo as it developed in there was fascinating.

**In 1990, the semi-conductor plant in Frankfurt (Oder) was more or less closed overnight. The monetary union (Germany-wide standardisation of currency) and the introduction of the Deutschmark meant that economic relations with the RGW (Rat für gegenseitige Wirtschaftshilfe, or Council for Mutual Economic Assistance) collapsed, and with it all exports. Do you remember the last time you were onsite?**

The mood was positive – nobody thought that the plant would close, myself included. But then suddenly, thousands were jobless. Nobody could comprehend why such a company was simply shut down. And the semi-conductor plant was not the only one. Bit by bit, the conglomerates of the GDR were liquidated. For the employees, it was a catastrophe. It also affected me. From one day to the next, the companies that commissioned my work were all gone. The photographic duplication of technical drawings became obsolete and I had to throw out huge amounts of film. Then I had to reorient myself. From 1990, countless housing lots, public buildings, and monuments were refurbished in Leipzig. The creditors required all refurbishments to be comprehensively documented. Through this, I found a new point of focus in my work.

## Robotron in Dresden: Contract Work, Urban Planning, Protests

Thomas Kübler is a historian, director of the Dresden City Archives and a professor at the Dresden Academy of Fine Arts. His research focuses on the history of the city of Dresden and on contract work in the GDR.

**From the 1960s onwards, the GDR recruited so-called contract workers through agreements with other socialist countries. In the years before the Berlin Wall was built, millions had left the GDR, creating a shortage of industrial labour. The Robotron combine was founded in 1969 and urgently needed workers. What role did contract labour play at Robotron?**

The agreements between socialist countries were made within the framework of the Council for Mutual Economic Assistance (CMEA). The Council was intended to tie Eastern European states more closely to the Soviet Union, with 'brother countries' such as Cuba and Vietnam added later. Under these agreements, people from these countries came to the GDR to help fill the labour shortage. The largest group of contract workers were Vietnamese. They were mainly employed in the textile industry or at the Fortschritt (progress) agricultural machinery combine, but not in the electronics sector. At that time, there was no established university system in North Vietnam. Hồ Chí Minh had other priorities – the country was very much shaped by agriculture. The workforce at Robotron was made up mainly of people from Hungary, as well as the USSR, Czechoslovakia and Bulgaria. The combine was not just involved in production; its primary focus was on development. Robotron pursued an active strategy to recruit highly qualified personnel. These countries had universities offering technical degrees, and there was an exchange programme with the Technical University (TH) in Dresden. In the 1960s, for example, many Bulgarian students came to Dresden to study cybernetics.

**In 1971, shortly after becoming General Secretary of the SED Central Committee, Erich Honecker declared cybernetics a pseudo-science. As a result, it also declined in importance at universities.**

Major political decisions often led to radical cutbacks in higher education policy. Honecker's push for the 'unity of economic and social policy', together with the large-scale housing construction programme, had a major impact on universities. As a result, teaching and research became increasingly centred on civil engineering and materials science.

**The agreements on contract labour in the GDR were concluded bilaterally and varied considerably. For example, Vietnamese contract workers received low wages and were housed in segregated dormitories, often under poor living and working conditions. Was the situation any different for the contract workers recruited by Robotron?**

They had a completely different status. Contract work often lasted only two years, after which workers were frequently offered permanent employment and stayed on. Robotron also made considerable efforts to support family reunification, something that was not available to contract workers from Vietnam, Angola, Mozambique, or Cuba. Their pay was on a par with that of GDR citizens, and attractive housing in Dresden was used to help recruit employees. The company newspaper was published in both German and Russian, as Russian was taught as a second language in all socialist countries. Overall, working conditions at Robotron were very good. In collaboration with the Central Institute for Nutrition, a research institute affiliated with the GDR Academy of Sciences, the company canteen offered employees a choice of six different meals.

**Technology and science were regarded as cornerstones of socialism's promise for the future. The new headquarters of the Robotron combine, completed in Dresden in the early 1970s, was a prime example. What significance did it hold from an urban planning and political perspective?**

Robotron was the GDR's most important combine. It was no coincidence that its director was a member of the Central Committee and deputy Minister of Economics. Under the slogan *Überholen ohne einzuholen* – 'overtake without ever needing to catch up' – the GDR set itself ambitious goals in microelectronics. With this motto, Walter Ulbricht expressed the aim of surpassing the Federal Republic of Germany in the technological race. The rationalisation and automation made possible by data processing were intended to transform the planned economy. The Robotron headquarters at Pirnaischer Platz was designed as a kind of campus, bringing together research, development and production management on a single site. This concept had already been implemented in the United States. The campus included facilities such as a kindergarten and a company canteen, which could be used as a venue for cultural events. The site was richly decorated with integrated artworks. A direct thoroughfare linked the vast Robotron complex on St. Petersburger Straße with the Prager Straße, which was designed in the same architectural style. The longest continuous residential building in the GDR was constructed here, with over 600 apartments, making a deliberate architectural statement. Its design was modelled on Le Corbusier's *Unité d'Habitation*. Many of the 'Robotroner,' as the employees called themselves, lived in these apartments. The entire complex was conceived as an integrated whole, presenting an idealised vision of the socialist city.

**Was this campus unique in the GDR?**

A similar campus was built around the same time in Jena, for the VEB Carl Zeiss Jena combine. As far as I am aware, these were the only two examples. In general, manufacturing industries were located outside major city centres, partly due to the risks posed by hazardous materials. In 1987, the Politburo approved the construction of a plant in Gittersee, on the outskirts of Dresden, to produce pure silicon, the essential material for semiconductor chips. This triggered a major environmental movement. Widespread protests quickly arose, ultimately forcing construction to be halted.

**The environmental movement drew attention to the massive pollution caused by state-owned enterprises and played a significant role in the Peaceful Revolution of 1989. How significant were the protests in Gittersee for the environmental movement in the GDR?**

These were the most significant protests of the environmental movement. Dresden's mayor, Wolfgang Berghofer, did not actively seek to suppress the movement. The city could hardly have done so, given that it had the highest rate of outmigration, dating back to the first major wave in 1984. In the wake of these events, an opposition network began to emerge. The environmental movement challenged the very raison d'être of the GDR, making it fundamentally different from, for example, today's climate movement. The protests against the high-purity silicon plant attracted international attention. They took place in the late 1980s, at a time when other socialist countries, such as Poland, Hungary, and Czechoslovakia, were already in deep crisis. All of this strengthened the movement against the plant. Alongside it, the campaign around the Kaditz sewage plant in Dresden, together with the church-based opposition, ultimately gave rise to the Peaceful Revolution.

## Gender Equality and Sexism at the Kombinat

Henrike Voigtländer is a historian and has completed her PhD at the Leibniz Centre for Contemporary History Potsdam and the Hannah Arendt Institute for Totalitarianism Studies in Dresden on *Sexism in the Workplace: Gender and Power in GDR Industry*.

**Your dissertation addresses the '*longue durée* of patriarchy in the GDR', as the summary puts it. You conducted research in the archives of various state-owned enterprises. Why there, specifically?**

State-owned enterprises, known as 'Volkseigene Betriebe' (VEBs), formed what researchers call the 'central nuclei of socialisation' in socialist East Germany. They provided social and cultural infrastructure, and organised childcare, leisure activities, and holidays. Even healthcare was organised through workplace-run polyclinics. Large industrial combines were responsible for allocating housing. Enterprises also implemented measures to promote women – the idea being that women would achieve equality primarily through paid employment. I focused on two major combines: the VEB Leuna Works and VEB Carl Zeiss Jena.

**To provide some context: the VEB Leuna Works was the largest enterprise in the GDR's chemical industry. VEB Carl Zeiss Jena was a leader in precision mechanics and optics, producing microscopes as well as military and space technology. The GDR's first computer, the Oprema, was built there in 1955. The combine also included the Dresden Microelectronics Research Centre (ZMD), where the 1-megabit chip U 61000 was developed.**

Carl Zeiss Jena had a large research division and its own commercial division. The combine regarded itself as an elite enterprise, whereas the Leuna Works saw itself more as a workers' combine. Crucially for my research, both enterprises had on-site units of the Ministry for State Security (MfS, commonly known as the Stasi). Embedding these units within enterprises allowed the MfS to monitor and steer the national economy. Foreign trade was also heavily surveilled. The files from these on-site MfS units, alongside company records and interviews, became a key source for my work.

**In the GDR, women were officially considered equal. The constitution enshrined not only their right to work but also their duty to do so. Yet alongside paid employment, women often performed domestic and care work alone – labour the ruling SED party did not recognise as work. In terms of qualifications, there was a clear gender hierarchy. In microelectronics, for example, women were overrepresented in production roles, while developers and engineers were predominantly men. What did you discover about gender equality in practice?**

There was undoubtedly a glass ceiling. Despite targeted qualification measures – such as psychological training programmes (what we would now call coaching) or special degree courses for women – women reached management positions far less often than men. Women were concentrated mainly in skilled and unskilled worker roles. By the 1980s, only around 20 percent of managerial positions in industrial enterprises were held by women. That is not insignificant, but it hardly reflected the official equality paradigm.

The development can be divided into three phases. In the early GDR, the initial goal was simply to bring women into paid employment. Around the 1960s, the focus shifted to qualifying women for skilled roles. Later still, greater emphasis was placed on reconciling work and family. Equality policies did create opportunities for women – workplace nurseries, for instance, made a real difference. Yet childcare remained a persistent problem; despite numerous initiatives, provision was never fully guaranteed. It is also worth noting that reaching management was not always attractive: these positions brought little extra pay and required SED membership.

My research confirmed my initial thesis: the equality paradigm did have an impact, but deeply entrenched sexism coexisted alongside it. By sexism, I mean an apparatus through which patriarchal power is maintained and reproduced. At senior levels in the combines, certain networks existed from which women were excluded. Using Stasi documents, I demonstrate that a conservative, patriarchal milieu operated within these circles – one that relied on sexist rhetoric, exchanged information about affairs, and procured sexual services on business trips. Women were not welcome in these networks.

**That sounds similar to the tech industry today, where 'tech bros' create an atmosphere of exclusion through exactly the bonding processes you describe: the group cultivates a sense of belonging through sexist remarks. Studies show that women who do break into development roles often feel so uncomfortable that they eventually leave the sector.**

Yes, that is a clear parallel. What was distinctive about the GDR was that the MfS existed – and with it, documentation that allows us to trace these practices today. At the same time, the MfS itself contributed to these dynamics by reinforcing and sustaining precisely these networks.

**From the 1970s onwards, many people from countries such as Vietnam and Angola worked in GDR enterprises as so-called 'contract workers' (Vertragsarbeiter*innen). What was their situation like?**

Migrant workers were subject to far stricter controls than their German colleagues, particularly regarding romantic and sexual relationships. They were housed in dormitories where overnight guests were prohibited. Women were not permitted to have children; if they became pregnant, they were required either to have an abortion or to return to their country of origin. Unlike their German colleagues, contract workers were also subjected to testing for sexually transmitted infections.

**Your sources also include texts produced in the 'circles of writing workers' (Zirkel schreibender Arbeiter), which were published in company magazines. These circles were part of socialist cultural policy under the 'Bitterfeld Way', an initiative intended to give working people access to art and artistic practice. What did you find in these texts?**

I was once asked whether the GDR simply lacked the time to achieve gender equality. Interestingly, however, the early years saw far more radical measures, which were later scaled back. One example was the idea of collectivising care work. The introduction of the 'baby year' in 1976 – allowing mothers to stay home for a year after giving birth – was something women had wanted, but it was also used exclusively by women. Many saw this as a step backwards for gender equality. Accordingly, gender equality featured more prominently in texts from the 1960s than in later decades. A typical storyline, for instance, centres on a woman who is new to the workplace and faces obstruction: male colleagues pile tasks on her, remarking that if she wants equality, she must perform equally. And performance, of course, was defined exclusively in terms of paid work.

**Work in the Kombinat: The Consequences of Automation**

Regina Bittner is a scholar of cultural studies and an ethnologist. She is deputy director of the Bauhaus Dessau Foundation and heads the Academy there. In the past, her research has focused on the structural transformation of the GDR's industrial landscape, and she has also contributed to exhibitions on the cultural history of workers.

**The introduction of microelectronics and increasing automation came with the promise of improved working conditions in state-owned enterprises. Was this promise fulfilled?**

At first glance, yes. For workers, the introduction of microelectronics and automation meant less dust, noise, dirt, and physical labour. But a closer look, supported by numerous studies, shows that existing conflicts in the workplace actually intensified. This was particularly true in relation to participation and co-determination within state-owned enterprises. In his publication on microelectronics in the GDR, Olaf Klenke vividly describes how economic and political pressure was passed down from the combine management to the workforce. Automation involved enormous investment costs, at a time when finances were already precarious. These costs were to be recovered by keeping the machines running continuously, which required shift work and the so-called 'rolling week'. This, in turn, led to resistance and petitions, as far as worker protests were possible in the GDR. Economic and political decisions made everyday life in the workplace more difficult, while simultaneously increasing the skill requirements for those operating the machines. The promise that technological progress would also bring social progress went unfulfilled.

**Investments in microelectronics created disparities between different industrial sectors. For example, Robotron benefited from a modern, campus-style headquarters in Dresden, while conditions at other industrial sites deteriorated.**

In the late GDR, there was a pronounced regional divide. Microelectronics sites increasingly became the focus of economic policy and received substantial investment – alongside Dresden, for example, in Jena and Erfurt. Meanwhile, in the heavy and chemical industries, there was a growing sense of being left behind. The infrastructure was falling apart, yet the machines were more or less kept running. Production continued regardless – almost in defiance of 'those at the top'.

**Unlike Western enterprises, East German enterprises were self-contained systems, capable of managing and maintaining their production independently.**

This was the result of a drive towards self-sufficiency. Cut off from global technological developments by the CoCom embargo and with limited resources, the GDR still sought to keep pace. Combines were designed as integrated units and, from the 1970s, operated across regions. The major enterprises had their own machine tool production and repair workshops. Not only that: they also shaped the social infrastructure, providing housing and holiday facilities. The enterprise was a social microcosm.

The microelectronics centres differed from other enterprises in that they relied on a workforce that was more highly educated and urban. This is particularly interesting, as it highlights the regional distribution of economic investment after 1990, with Dresden emerging as the heart of 'Silicon Saxony'.

**From the 1970s onwards, new urban centres developed and everyday life in the GDR began to change. Did this also bring a shift in attitudes towards work?**

Under Honecker's agenda of the 'unity of economic and social policy,' the early 1970s saw efforts to raise living standards in the GDR and improve people's sense of well-being. The political regime needed to legitimise itself, and increasing the production of consumer goods was intended to help. The combines were suddenly expected to produce consumer goods in addition to their regular output. Western cultural products, such as films and pop music, were now tolerated, and leisure activities became more important. Large cultural centres were built, such as the Stadthalle in Chemnitz (1974) and the Palast der Republik in Berlin (1976). In Dresden, the Kulturpalast had already opened in 1969. The focus was no longer solely on shaping the socialist personality from above; popular and leisure culture were now seen as a way to allow individual freedom. The socialist personality was to develop not only through work, but also during leisure time. The idea of integration through work was beginning to falter.

**Did this also have an impact on the development of enterprises?**

The original idea was that work would integrate individuals into society. However, by the 1980s, the emphasis had increasingly shifted towards individualisation. This development had a postmodern twist, if one can speak of postmodernism in the context of the GDR. The relationship between the individual and society played an important role in the social science discourse of the time. The focus was now solely on the convergence of social classes and strata, rather than on their seamless alignment. This marked a significant shift in perspective.

Automation was associated with particular ideas about management. In theory, this was known as 'post-Fordism,' meaning a shift away from assembly-line work towards team-based ways of working. The so-called human relations approach was also adopted in the East. Flexible management was intended to give workers greater opportunities for participation and involvement. These management concepts were also discussed within the GDR's combines. At the same time, demands for greater participation by workers often contrasted with the reality of low wages and the pressures of shift work. As a result, tensions continued to rise and were expressed through a refusal to work, or at least a reluctance to maintain high levels of performance. Attempts to adapt western management concepts to socialist principles ultimately failed.

**What effect did this have on the period of transformation in the 1990s?**

My argument is – and the literature on social, societal, and economic transformations after 1990 supports this – that the factory directors and functionaries in the late GDR, and more broadly across Eastern Europe, who had already been using these new management techniques from the 1980s, were the very same people who later played a leading role in advancing the political agenda of privatisation and the dismantling of state-owned enterprises. One example of this is the economist and politician Václav Klaus from what was then Czechoslovakia. He pursued a capitalist privatisation agenda, leaving little room for alternative perspectives.

## Robotron 1990: Liquidation and New Beginnings

Rolf Heinemann forefronted the database development of the Robotron combine, and was also a competitive athlete in the GDR. In 1990, together with other former Robotron employees, he founded a new company. Located in Dresden, Robotron Datenbank-Software GmbH still successfully operates today.

**From 1965, you worked for the Institut für Datenverarbeitung (Institute for Data Processing), a predecessor of the Robotron conglomerate. When Robotron was founded in 1969, you become an employee. Did you view that as an opportunity?**

For me, it was certainly an opportune moment. Together with a colleague, I was working at the Institute for Data Processing on a software system that ran on the Robotron mainframe computer, the R300. The focus here was the operative system for production preparation, more specifically the automated administration of bills of materials. Then came the huge turning-point: the Institute for Data Processing was integrated into the Robotron conglomerate, which was founded on 1 April 1969. At the time, IBM's assembly language was setting the pace worldwide. As a consequence, the programming language of the R300 no longer met international standards. This led to the introduction of ESER, an integrated system for electronic computing technologies. ESER emerged due to the cooperation of a number of socialist countries. The 1970s saw the market entry of the Robotron product R21, followed by the more developed models E40 to E57: the first mainframe computers of the ESER system. For them, we developed the first database system, DBSR. To be sure, there were some precursors, but ultimately, we programmed DBSR from scratch. From that point on, things moved fast. Robotron grew at a rapid pace. The new centre was built in Dresden, and we had the possibility to engage more employees.

**How well-informed were you about international standards, for example in the development of databases?**

We had an Information Department. I would register what I needed there, for example technical literature. Everything we requested, we got – even source code for software systems. Through this, it was possible to maintain an overview of developments in the international world of database software. The US-American companies – Oracle, IBM, the Digital Equipment Corporation – were the pioneers. To begin with, we were able to develop our own technology. But in 1985, the Robotron management approached me to say that we had to adapt to Digital Equipment. The technology was smuggled in and we had to develop a database for it fast. We had two years and a team of just 100 people to achieve what Oracle had created with 8,000 people and five years. That was impossible, so we adapted pre-existing systems. I pushed for us to replicate the Oracle software. At the time, Oracle was a global market leader.

**As events in 1990 unfolded and it became clear that the two German states would unify, was it clear to you that the GDR conglomerates would have to reposition themselves?**

Through my activity as an orienteering athlete, I was able to frequently travel and had good relations to people abroad. I knew that we would have to adapt if we were to keep pace. In the field of hardware, we didn't stand a chance. But in the field of software, I saw a possibility. The unification came much sooner than anticipated. By the time that Cebit – at the time one of the largest trade fairs for information technology – came along in the spring of 1990, I was already looking for a partner among the Western database companies in order to establish a new company. Asthon-Tate, IBM, and Siemens rejected my proposal. For them, forming a new company in the East was not an option. The colleagues at Siemens even told me that there was no way I could know what a database was. In the end, I landed at Oracle. I knew the system there very well of course, because we had originally adapted it to ours. They were aware of that and agreed to a cooperation immediately.

**How did you found your company?**

It wasn't easy to find employees. Many had already been acquired by Western companies such as SAP. But I was able to convince 28 people to stay in Dresden. The state-owned Robotron conglomerate was liquidated by the Treuhand (the state trust agency responsible for privatisation). I was able to secure a credit from the interim administration, and also had to contribute capital myself. In August 1990, following the monetary union (the Germany-wide standardisation of currency), we were able to found the company 'Robotron Datenbank Software GmbH' with an initial investment of 65,000 Deutschmark. The managing director of Oracle Deutschland at the time, Franz Niedermaier, supported us immensely, because he recognised that a cooperation would represent a win-win situation for Oracle, too. During the GDR period, we had supplied the economy's 32 most important enterprises with our adapted version of the Oracle software. Niedermaier offered me the right to distribute the official Oracle license, which provided the company with an immediate source of income. Our first client was the Nationale Volksarmee (National People's Army) of the GDR. Within six months, the company was already making a profit. I had very good programmers; alongside distribution, our maintenance service for companies in East and West Germany was an important source of income. Back then, there were hardly any technicians around who were able to service Oracle products, but they were very much in demand. Our clients even included the largest bank in Switzerland.

**Did you experience difficulties with the Treuhand when establishing the company?**

No, that was all sorted out by the head of the finance department of the conglomerate as it was being liquidated. In my view, the discontinuation of Robotron's software branch, which was worth 28 million and was well-positioned to compete, was a huge failure of the Treuhand. The second big mistake was the termination of the managing director, Hans-Jürgen Lodahl, apparently for political reasons. He went over to Siemens and was replaced with Peter Adenauer, the grandson of Konrad Adenauer, who essentially had no idea what he was doing. It didn't take him long to drive the remaining operation into insolvency.

**How did the company develop from that point on?**

We intensified our cooperation with Oracle and won another big contract. Oracle wanted to enter the Russian market with a Russian-language version. Three of my people worked for two years to adapt the program accordingly. In the meantime, we had taken on the company acronym of RDS – Robotron Datenbank Software GmbH. We also used this acronym for our logo. I was concerned that the name would be too easily associated with the socialist period. But a conversation with the marketing director of Oracle convinced me to hold on to the name of Robotron. He said: 'Three letters – that isn't a proper name for a company. We have 8,000 developers here, and the majority of them probably don't even know that there were two German states. They hardly know where Europe is. But if I ask what Robotron is, half of them will know that it's a company in the East – in fact the only one that can keep pace with us.'

**How did you secure the name 'Robotron'?**

In 1994, I approached the Treuhand, which had set up an administrative body for the liquidation of Robotron operations. I had a directive from the former managing director of Robotron stipulating that companies which had developed out of Robotron could retain the brand. However, the directive was not legally binding. So I called the Trademark Office in Munich. They proceeded to tell me that the brand belonged to the Robotron conglomerate, which of course no longer existed. But apparently it had patented the brand back in 1987 – for a ten-year period. So in 1997, I called Munich again. The patent had expired. It cost 200 Deutschmark to have the listing annulled and reapply to acquire the name.

# Antye Guenther



Due to the CoCom embargo, hardly any relevant computer technology found its way into socialist states during the Cold War – at least not through official channels. The Stasi persuaded the Japanese chip manufacturer Toshiba, among others, to smuggle plans and components into the GDR. Eventually, the Centre for Microelectronics Dresden (ZMD) was able to develop the 1-megabit chip in collaboration with VEB Carl Zeiss Jena. In 1988, it was ceremoniously presented to Erich Honecker. According to legend, the Toshiba managers were rewarded not only with large sums of money, but also with Meissen porcelain. The chip never entered serial production in the GDR. Antye Guenther takes the Toshiba scandal as the starting point for a speculative artwork. A coffee service becomes a secret data carrier for highly sensitive information, combining original Stasi files with fictional research material. The artist transposed elements of the chip's design plan into the Blue Onion pattern of the porcelain using glaze. Other pieces were produced in collaboration with the porcelain painters at the Meissen manufactory.

Operation ZWIEBELMUSTER (Operation Blue Onion)
2021–25 | Coffee service, Meissen porcelain, 28 pieces; Blue Onion pattern with partially multi-layered platinum overglaze; six unique pieces with a modified Blue Onion design based on the artist's drawings; documents; 1-megabit chip layout plan; performance with image and research material | Dimensions variable

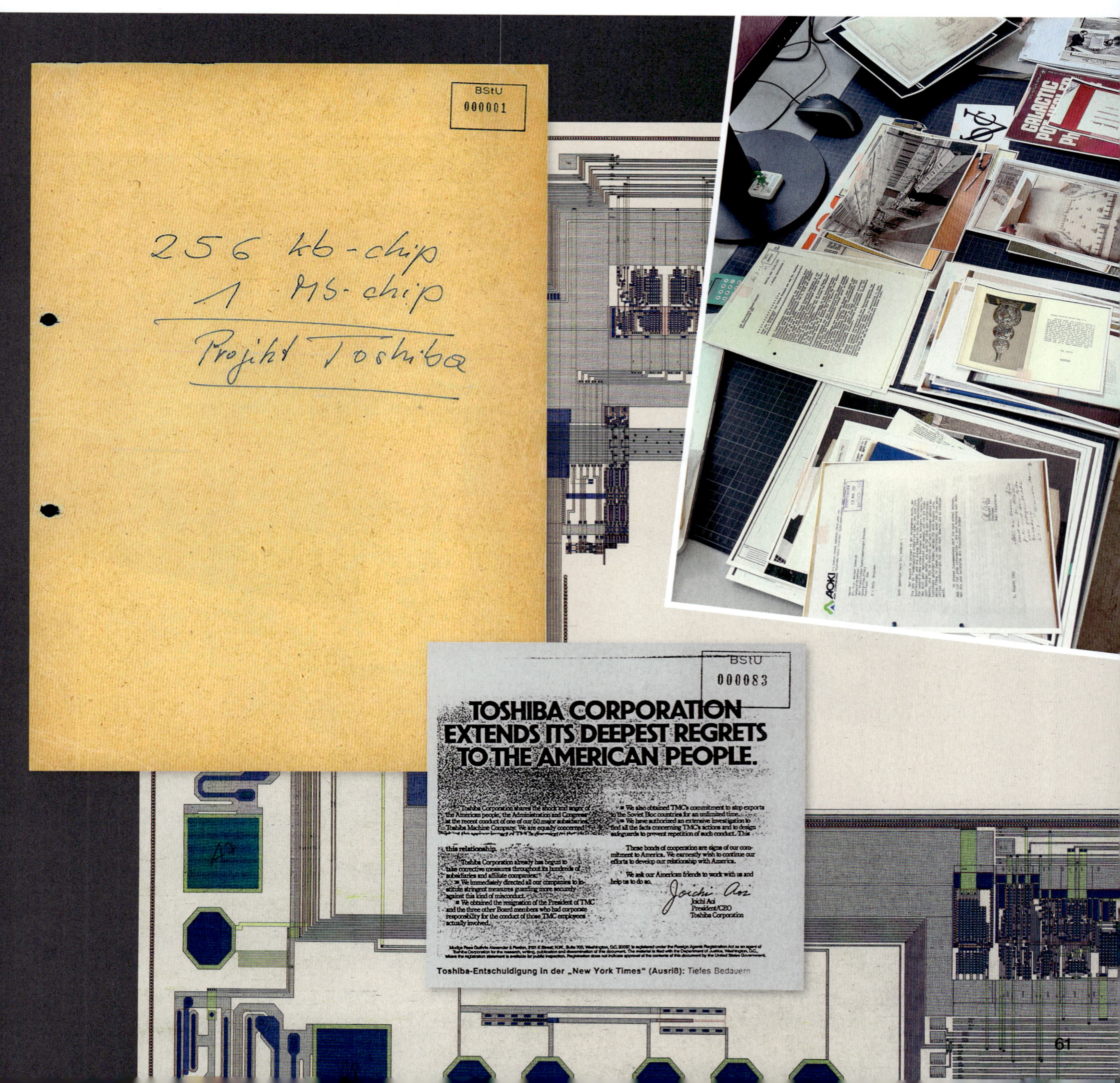

DIE DDR IST RICHTG PROGRAMM

Hauptabteilung XVIII
Major/ Gen. ▮▮▮▮▮

Berlin, 15. Mai 1986

BStU
000006

MfS
- 336 -
2 0 MAI 1986

Ministerium für
Staatssicherheit Berlin
Leiter der Hauptabteilung XVIII
Generalmajor ▮▮▮▮▮

Betr: Zur möglichen Zwingerkopie in Arita, Japan und die
Nutzbarmachung für operative Vorgänge

Lieber Genosse ▮▮▮▮▮,
wie Sie bereits wissen, sind wir seit längerem auf der Suche nach potentiellen
Trainingsstätten für zukünftig anzuwerbende Kundschafter des Friedens
im NSW. Für den für uns so wichtigen japanischen Raum scheint sich nun eine
Möglichkeit aufzutun (siehe Bericht IMS Barock). Eine angestrebte
Zwingerkopie im südlichen Kushu würde nicht nur die für eine bestmögliche
Schulung der angeworbenen Personen nötige typisch-europäische Architektur
und Innenausstattung garantieren. Aufgrund der Abgeschiedenheit wäre dieser
Neubau auch einem deutlich geringeren Fremdenttarnungsrisiko ausgesetzt.
Wir wissen bereits, dass touristische Freizeitaktivitätskulissen sehr gut
geeignet sind, operative Vorgänge effektiv zu maskieren. Hinzu kommt, daß
wir im Dresdner Zwinger bereits mehrere operative Übergabeorte etablieren
konnten, und sich damit die einzigartige Möglichkeit ergeben würde,
festgelegte Kontrollmaßnahmen etc in gespiegelten Räumlichkeiten vor Ort in
Japan unter semi-realen Bedingungen trainieren zu können. Ich würde dies
gerne demnächst persönlich mit Ihnen und Gen. ▮▮▮▮▮ besprechen. Im
Anschluss daran könnten wir mit der nächsten Arita Delegation noch in ▮▮▮
Jahr den Auftrag auslösen, vor Ort mögliche Kontaktpersonen aus▮▮▮
machen.

gez. ▮▮▮▮▮

Grundriss
0,55
0,55
1,23
1,20
Bearbeitung

3
Arbeitsgruppe BKK
Berlin, 22. Dezember 1987
Tgb.-Nr.: 2791 /87
rec-br
BStU
000065
Hauptverwaltung A
SWT/XIV
Leiter
Bezug nehmend auf unser Schreiben vom 5. 12. 1987, Tgb.
übersenden wir Ihrer Diensteinheit einen weiteren Gesp
über Darlegungen eines führenden Vertreters des japani
Toshiba über nachrichtendienstlich gesteuerte Überprü
lich der Verletzung der Embargobestimmungen der USA d
bei Lieferungen in die DDR zur operativen Auswertung
Verbleib.
Leiter der Ar
Meinel
Oberst
Anlage
BSTU
0013
2
Er erwartet auf alle Fälle während des nächsten Besuches in
Tokyo das Kaffeeservice aus Meißner Porzellan. Auf den Geld-
betrag von 10000 Dollar, den er nannte, von mir angesprochen
und auch dabei zum Ausdruck gebracht, daß eine Übergabe in
Berlin möglich sei, wurde von ihm erneut verständlich gemacht,
daß er diese Leistungen in Tokyo erbracht haben möchte, um
offensichtlich allen Erschwernissen und Gefahren aus dem Wege
zu gehen. Er gab zu verstehen, daß er für den Fall des vorher
erfolgten Zusammentreffens meinerseits mit Kovo den Geldbe-
trag während des nächsten Besuches erwartet. Das Problem Ikonen
wurde von ihm nicht erneut angesprochen.
brachte zum Ausdruck, daß er erwartet, daß alle Fragen
Geschäftes zwischen KME und Toshiba und alle auftretenden
me nur von meiner Seite als Vertreter KME und von seiner
Toshiba zwischen uns beiden geklärt bzw. vorbehandelt
müßten. Er brachte zum Ausdruck, daß auch auf höchster
Ebene, z. B. in Form von Gesprächen zwischen Dr.
und Dr. Nagai nur das vereinbart werden könnte, was
zwischen uns abgestimmt und abgesprochen sei. Er halte
solche Zusammentreffen zwischen Dr. Nagai und Dr. Wedler
zweckmäßig und notwendig, aber man solle zum Inhalt der
äfte keine Wunder erwarten, da die Mentalität und Ge-
en in japanischen Firmen so sei, daß ein einzelner
Vertreter niemals Zugeständnisse oder Kompro-
vorher nicht mit der darunterliegenden
e abgestimmt sei. Es würden also
auch die Repräsentanzebene jeweils
ein. In den Gesprächen wurde von
daß man mit dem Vorgehen von Mr.
sehr vorsichtig sein müsse,
im Auftrage von Dr. Nagai handelnd
eichzeitig wurde aber von ▇ zum
ie Fa. O:A. Maschinery nach wie
a sehr enge Beziehungen zwischen
inerseits und andererseits Dr.
BA
ZMD U61000C
B12 A2

Bild 11
Querschnitt
n-Transistor
(Randelektronik)

Bild 12
Querschliff
-Poly-Si-1-Leitbahn
-Al/n+ -Kontakt

# Helga Paris

In 1981 and 1982, Helga Paris took photographs in Leipzig's main railway station. The place was often bustling, especially during the Leipzig Trade Fair, which attracted visitors from around 100 countries. This showcase of the GDR's economy also presented the latest products in computer technology and microelectronics. Posters of the VEB Kombinat Robotron shine brightly on two glass block walls in the station, depicting people at work on data processing machines and computers. Travellers hurry towards the platforms or wait in the halls for their trains. Perhaps we also glimpse a few commuters on their way to one of the region's industrial combines. Paris' images come together to form a unique portrait of GDR society, quite unlike the one suggested in the pictorial tableaux of Socialist Realism. This is a society that is assertive and defiant. People discover loopholes in the system, moments of freedom. Their inner lives remain concealed.

Leipzig Hauptbahnhof (Leipzig Central Station)
1981/82 | B/w photographs | 24×33 cm

robotron

WERKZEUGMASCHINEN
FERTIGUNGSANLAGEN
Schnellzug
9 30
Dresden Hbf
Gleis
19

History is often narrated as social history: the succession of power shifts, crises, wars, uprisings, and reforms. Would the development of the GDR be clearer if viewed through the lens of economic history? From the outset, its economy was shaped by political intervention and the idea of central planning. Yet it was never free from the logic of the market. Internally, the GDR shielded itself from it; externally, it still had to adapt to it, submit to it, and succeed or fail with its products on the world market. The Socialist Unity Party (SED) feared the loss of control this would bring, but by the early 1980s it was impossible to detach from global market forces or to ignore them altogether. Turning a blind eye to this economic reality did nothing to change it.

From the late 1960s onwards, the development of microelectronic components progressed worldwide with increasing dynamism, both in terms of the diversity of functions and storage capacity. This reflects the extent to which research and industrial capacity were concentrated in this field. A growing number of functional elements were integrated into an ever smaller area. This led to an enormous increase in capacity. The 8-bit memory chip manufactured in 1968 could retain just a single character; by the early 1990s, the leading 4-megabit chip could already store 300 typewritten pages. Within a quarter of a century, storage capacity thus increased by a factor of 500,000.

Alongside a high degree of circuit complexity, minimal dimensions, and high reliability, integration technology also achieved a level of economic viability that had previously been unthinkable. 'A particularly vivid example of the consequences of miniaturisation and falling prices is provided by the development of the computer. One of the first computers was built in the USA in 1940. It consisted of 18,000 valves, weighed 30 tonnes, cost 2 million US dollars, was housed on an area of 140 m², and consumed 150 kW (roughly the output of a medium-sized shunting locomotive). The emergence of more affordable and more powerful microprocessors – small centres of information processing – resolved the problem of cost, size, and function from the 1970s onwards. Thus, by the end of the 1970s, a silicon chip contained more functional elements than the first American computer. The chip was twenty times faster, had a larger memory, was a thousand times more reliable, consumed considerably less power, required one thirty-thousandth of the volume, and cost only one ten-thousandth of the original device.' (Olaf Klenke)

# What Is History?

In his 1972 essay 'Return to History', the French philosopher Michel Foucault describes the relationship between historiography and structuralism. He emphasises the need to develop a better understanding of the diversity of historical events and developments:

'[…] In traditional history it was thought that events were what was known, what was visible, what was directly or indirectly identifiable, and the work of the historian was to search for their cause or their meaning. The event, on the other hand, was essentially visible, even if one sometimes lacked the documents to establish it with certainty. Serial history makes it possible to bring out different layers of events as it were, some being visible, even immediately knowable by the contemporaries, and then, beneath these events that form the froth of history, so to speak, there are other events that are invisible, imperceptible for the contemporaries, and are of completely different form. […] Beneath this layer of events, there exists another type of events that are a bit more diffuse – events that are not perceived exactly in the same way by the contemporaries, but which they have a certain awareness of all the same, for example, a lowering or an increase in prices which will change their economic behavior. And then, beneath these events as well, you have others that are hard to locate, that are often barely perceptible for the contemporaries but nonetheless constitute decisive breaks. Thus the reversal of a trend, the point at which an economic curve that had been increasing levels off or begins to decline, such a point is a very important event in the history of a town, a country, or possibly a civilization, but the people who are its contemporaries are not aware of it. […] It is history's task to uncover this hidden layer of diffuse, "atmospheric", polycephalic events that determine, finally and profoundly, the history of the world. For it is quite clear to us now that the reversal of an economic trend is much more important than the death of a king.'

# Events of Long Duration

# The Stasi as an Economic Factor

In November 1949, the Coordinating Committee on Multilateral Export Controls (CoCom) was founded in Paris. This informal advisory and coordinating body was used by the United States and its allies to control the export of technology to Eastern Bloc states. As reinforced in a US law from 1962: 'It is the policy of the United States to use its economic resources and advantages in trade with Communist-dominated nations to further the national security and foreign policy objectives of the United States.'

CoCom drew up a list of goods that could not be exported to the Eastern Bloc. These included weapons, nuclear technology, industrial plants, and microelectronics. The export controls were intended to prevent the transfer of key technologies and thereby secure both military and economic advantages in the Cold War, as the 'technological battle' was regarded as a crucial arena of confrontation between the blocs. The CoCom list was repeatedly updated – older technologies were cleared for export to the East, while new, strategically significant technologies and goods were added and embargoed. The main enforcement mechanism was sanctions against companies that violated CoCom regulations.

For the development of microelectronics in East Germany, the CoCom list posed a major obstacle, as it excluded the country from global networks of research, development, and production – not only in terms of patents and licences but also with regard to technical equipment, microelectronic components, and the latest innovations in computer technology.

# Embargo Policy and Illegal Imports

In the 1980s, technological progress worldwide led to a fundamental change in production methods. No state had the economic resources to shoulder the rising development costs in microelectronics on its own. International division of labour was now seen as the only way to limit financial risks and remain competitive amid accelerating technological change.

The GDR, excluded from direct access to Western technologies by the embargo, increasingly had to 'reinvent' them. Illegal technology transfers were handled mainly by the Stasi (East Germany's Ministry for State Security) and the Department for Commercial Coordination within the Ministry of Foreign Trade. Subsidiary companies were established abroad – in Switzerland and Austria, as well as in Japan, South Korea, and Taiwan – through which the GDR was able to purchase goods that appeared on the embargo list. At the same time, the Stasi sought to gain insight into Western technological development through industrial espionage in companies and research institutes. Its operations were often economically profitable; they sometimes shortened research and development times considerably, helping the East German economy to continue producing competitive goods for international markets.

Imports of Western technology often served as the starting point for domestic innovation. It was the import of several hundred high-performance computers with 16- and 32-bit technology between 1985 and 1988 that made it possible to introduce CAD/CAM (computer-aided design and manufacturing) and laid the foundation for Robotron's development of more powerful computers.

In his book on microelectronics in the GDR, the science historian Gerhard Barkleit traces how the GDR moved from a 'dual bureaucracy' – in which the economy was directed both by the SED and its leadership bodies and by the state administration – towards a 'triple bureaucracy', especially in the field of advanced technologies, in which the State Security (Stasi) also exerted influence on economic decisions. By the 1980s, nothing could be done without it. State Security had become a 'strategic cross-cutting institution' with 'considerable covert capacity to steer and manipulate', which, he argues, 'made a significant stabilising contribution to the GDR's system of state and economic organisation'. Its growing influence was evident both in the illicit procurement of specialised microelectronics equipment and in appointments to senior posts in enterprises. Often, the intelligence service emerged as the 'most realistic' actor within this triad of power. Accordingly, even ahead of major investment decisions, the Stasi sought to exert influence in order to identify political 'wishful dreams' at an early stage and prevent misinvestment.

# Horst Bartnig

Horst Bartnig (1936–2025) was a representative of Concrete Art in Germany. This was by no means a straightforward choice in the GDR, where official art policy favoured idealised images of work and everyday life and discouraged abstraction. Bartnig began creating abstract works as early as the 1960s, turning to computer-generated graphics from the late 1970s. At the mainframe computer of the Central Institute for Information Processing of the GDR Academy of Sciences in East Berlin, he collaborated with scientists to generate variations of form and colour, which he then translated into groups of works. His questions are closely linked to those of information theory and cybernetics. Chance and personal signature are deliberately excluded from his practice. He most often exhibited his work outside the official state art system – at private shows, at the Rossendorf Nuclear Research Centre, or at the Arkade Gallery in Berlin.

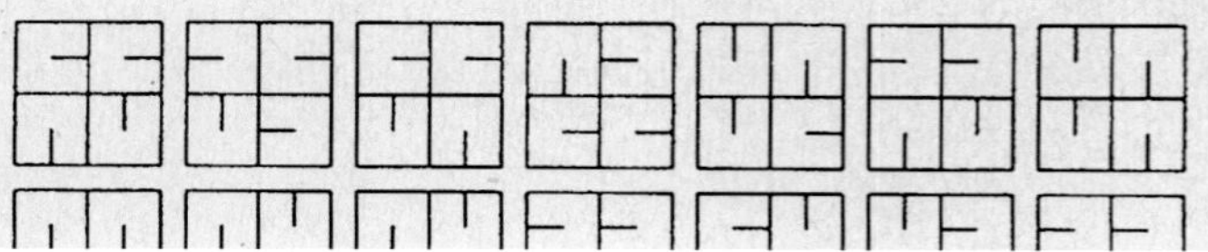

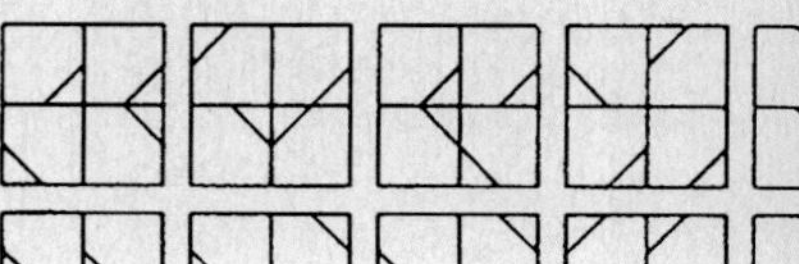

3622 Variationen (3622 Variations)
1984/85 | Computer-generated graphics, hand-printed line etching | 4 sheets, 94.5×74.5 cm

# Marion Wenzel

In 1989, the Leipzig photographer Marion Wenzel visited the VEB Semiconductor Plant Frankfurt (Oder). Just a year later, the production of microchips and transistors was to be discontinued. At this moment, however, they were still being manufactured – for the GDR, the Soviet Union, and countries such as Poland, Romania, and Czechoslovakia. Most of the factory workers were women. The sensitive semiconductor technology was manufactured in so-called 'clean rooms', environments where not a single particle of dust could be allowed to enter. Workers could access them only by passing through an airlock. Before doing so, they put on special protective suits and head covering. Much of Wenzel's artistic work focuses on photographing the changes in the landscape around Leipzig arising from lignite mining. She visited the factory as part of a pleinair event together with other artists. She photographed a series of images in medium format and with direct flash to create proximity, capture details, and describe the working situation with highly sensitive technology. Before she could expand the series, the semiconductor plant was liquidated.

From the series: Pleinair Mikroelektronik Frankfurt (Oder)
1989 | Baryte prints | 38.7×57.6 cm | 46.5×56.3 cm | 58.1×39 cm | 38.6×57.4 cm

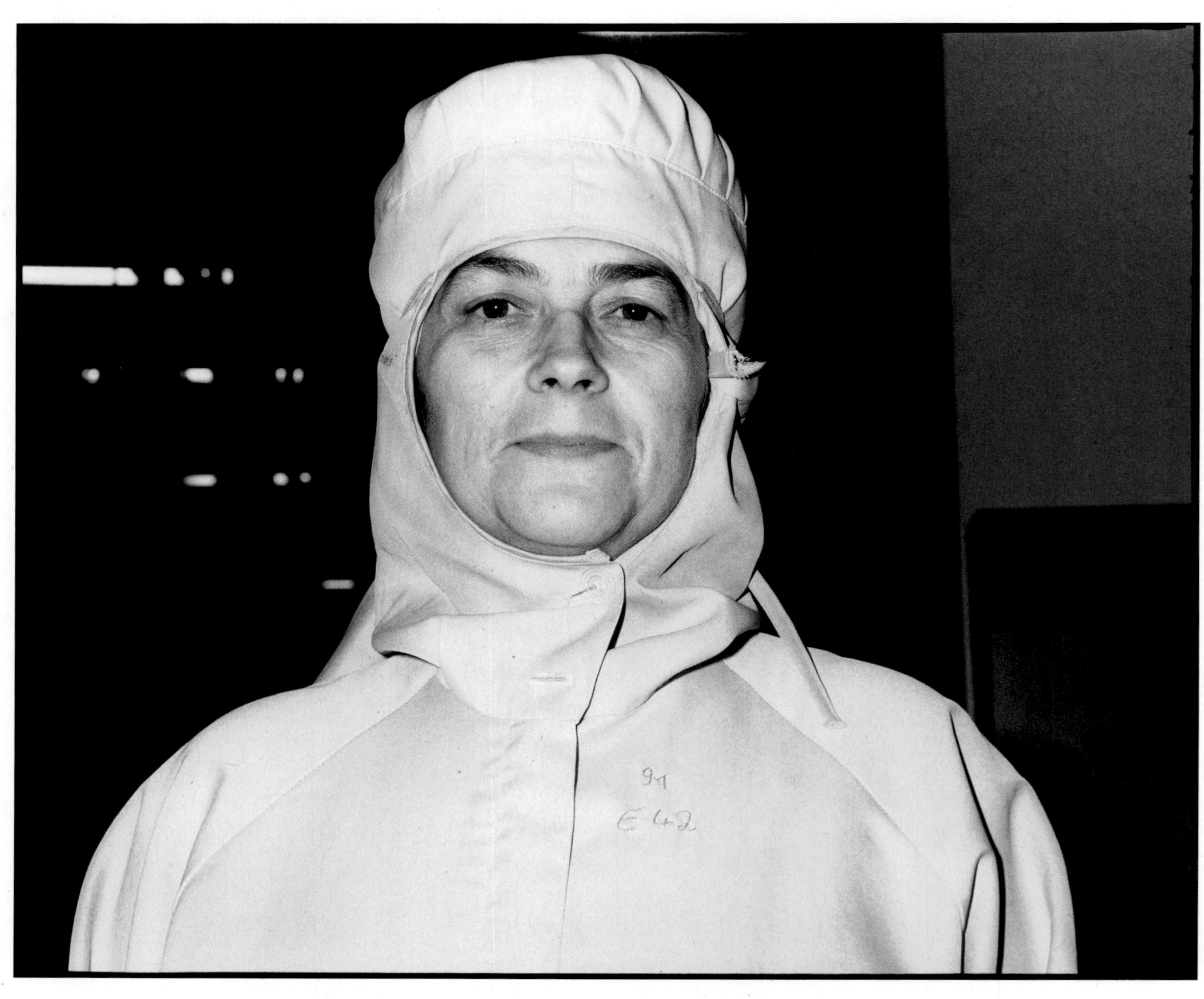

The decision to build up a microelectronics industry in the GDR in 1977 put the sector under pressure to rapidly increase silicon production. This led to a striking accumulation of accidents in the chemical departments of the semiconductor industry. At VEB Spurenmetalle Freiberg, a 'mass accident' occurred in November 1977, followed by an explosion just one month later. In both cases, workers suffered chemical burns to the skin and respiratory tract due to escaping trichlorosilane, which is required for the production of high-purity silicon. Trichlorosilane is considered highly flammable and, after rapid evaporation, forms highly toxic hydrogen chloride fumes, the lethal concentration of which is very low at approximately one gram per cubic metre.

In March 1978, a fire broke out in the department for the chemical production of circuit boards at VEB Messelektronik Berlin, in which workers suffered severe burns from the released chlorine gas. Silicon production was a dangerous field of work; even as late as the end of the 1980s, the Stasi estimated the risk of accidents in this production sector to be high.

# Clean Room

The term 'clean room' suggests that the manufacture of microchips is a particularly clean technology. That is an illusion: the clean room protects the chips from dust, but not the workers. While the room air is constantly circulated to ensure the purity of the silicon wafers, the chemical-intensive manufacturing process simultaneously contaminates the air and endangers the health of the workers. In a study conducted in the production area for microelectronic components at the Halbleiterwerk (Semiconductor Works) in Frankfurt (Oder) in the mid-1980s, more than half of the employees found the working conditions burdensome. The artificial ventilation created an unpleasant overpressure, and the noise level of the air conditioning system was often only slightly below the maximum statutory limits. The employees, mostly women, frequently complained of fatigue, exhaustion, and a feeling of dryness in the mouth. Difficulty falling asleep and staying asleep, lethargy, sensitivity to noise, nausea, and strong heart palpitations were also often cited as health consequences of the working conditions in the clean room, which is why occupational scientists in the GDR assumed that only young people could cope with these working conditions for a relatively short period of time.

# Mental Taylorism

Work in chip manufacturing was defined by monotonous, simple, and repetitive work processes. In the field of photolithography, for example, the following movements were constantly repeated: the silicon wafer is taken from the magazine with a pipette; it is placed on the alignment plate; the position is checked under the microscope and corrected if necessary; subsequently, the wafer is exposed and returned to the tray in the stack magazine. The entire process repeats itself several hundred times per shift.

Computer work was not automatically considered versatile and intellectually demanding. Often, work remained monotonous and uniform even with the new technology. This was because a fundamental organisational principle of industrial labour had not changed at all: the principle of the Taylorist fragmentation of labour, with its often monotonous specialisation – which had proven particularly effective since the beginning of the 20th century – continued in the factories even with the new technology. 'After more than a decade of promoting microelectronics in the GDR, practically every aspect of work showed that, even with the introduction of new technologies, the work process was structured according to economic requirements and not according to the needs of human labour power. Without a change in the social conditions under which the new technology was applied, no new character of work developed either.' (Olaf Klenke)

# New Technology, Old Work

In February 1986, the VEB Kombinat Carl Zeiss Jena took the lead in the GDR's chip development. Researchers from the Central Research Centre for Microelectronics in Dresden, who had made a name for themselves with the development of the 4-kilobit SRAM chip, were summoned to Jena. After a lavish breakfast, Carl Zeiss General Director Wolfgang Biermann announced that, following a decision by the SED leadership, the Dresden research centre would, with immediate effect, be placed under the Carl Zeiss combine.

Biermann instructed them to produce, without delay, a plan that would keep the GDR in step with international developments. He outlined three tasks: the fastest possible transition to series production of the 256-kilobit memory; pilot production of the 1-megabit DRAM memory by 1989; and of the 4-megabit chip by 1992/93. Only once the plan was finished would the Dresden team be allowed to leave the Jena guesthouse.

The experts sat together day and night, debating heatedly over their concept as it gradually came together: What do we have, what do we need, what could we develop ourselves, what will the Soviet Union supply, what will it cost? Those were the questions at stake. Each evening, Biermann would appear, expecting a report. After two weeks, the 'Programme for Very Large-Scale Integration' was in place.

Packing two million components onto a chip the size of a fingernail was a formidable challenge for the scientists from Dresden. The embargo made many things more difficult; at the same time, they had a solid grasp of how the memory should be developed, and much of the circuitry had already been tried and tested, so the task was chiefly one of systematic scientific development. To speed up development, the Stasi supplied documentation for a Japanese 1-megabit chip, but for the Dresden team it was useless: it did not fit their approach or their technical set-up. Their biggest problem was getting hold of the right machines. Around 100 were needed to manufacture a chip. The GDR and the Soviet Union could supply roughly half the required production equipment; the rest, because of the embargo, could be obtained only through illegal channels.

On 9 August 1988, they produced their first fault-free 1-megabit chip. A few weeks later, General Director Biermann presented it to Erich Honecker as proof of the GDR economy's capabilities.

In 1989, limited series production began in Dresden, and several tens of thousands of 1-megabit memory chips could be supplied to Robotron. But the machines needed for mass production were not available. For development, despite the embargo, it had been possible to bring a few units into the GDR; now, however, hundreds would have been required.

# The World as Will and Representation

# 1-Megabit Chip

Just one day after the GDR had publicly unveiled its 1-megabit chip, the CIA appeared at Siemens in Munich. The US intelligence service did not believe the chip was a GDR in-house development and set out to find a leak at Siemens. For days, they pored over files – without success. The CIA found nothing – because there was nothing to find Klaus Garbrecht, who at the time led Siemens's 1-megabit project, recalled: 'For many, the GDR's megabit chip was something like a small Sputnik shock.'

# Is it possible to escape the world market?

The pressure to innovate means that an economy must keep pace with technological advances and help shape them through research and development in order to produce goods that can compete on the world market.

To keep up in the field of microelectronics, the GDR invested enormous sums during the 1980s. This concentration of resources left other sectors without the funds needed for modernisation. As a result, problems with wear and tear, spare parts supply, and the replacement of outdated equipment became so severe that many industries – above all the chemical sector – were barely manageable. These one-sided investment decisions turned the GDR's economy during the 1980s into a 'prisoner of the world economy'.

# knowbotiq

Three 'metallurgical phantoms' drift through the clean rooms contained within the glove boxes: tungsten, tantalum, and gallium. These chemical elements are essential for the production of computer chips. They are extracted primarily in China (tungsten, gallium) and the Congo (tantalum), often under precarious conditions. In contrast, technology is always marketed with the pledge of happiness. Yet within the sterile clean rooms of chip production, the three metals stir 'alien affects' that unsettle these carefully manufactured promises. Gallium, with its liquid consciousness, proclaims 'This clean room is solving for happy', echoing a phrase from the former Google X executive Mo Gawdat. Tantalum responds by invoking a concept developed by the scholar Sara Ahmed, which gives the work its title. 'Refusing to "be happy" in a broken world is not failure. This is solidarity.' And it calls out to us: 'Be the killjoy. The one who doesn't fit. The one who doesn't forget. The one who remembers the others. You are not failing. The system is.'

Clean Room affect.aliens
2025 | Glove boxes made from recycled agricultural films, e-papers, PVC pipes, Raspberry Pi, tab | Sound: Pablo Torres

**Glove Box 1 — Gallium**

**Entry cue** (*clean room voice*):
ISO Class 1 clean room.

Cooling cycle active.
55%. Micro-particle flush
in progress.

Noise threshold: <50dB.

Emotion: not specified.

Please, proceed to airlock.
Stop.
Stand still.
Air shower in progress.

Particles removed: skin
cells, hair, fibers, dust.

**Voice of Gallium** (*fluid awareness, patient*):
Hide your skin. Hide your smell.

Come closer —
I have already spread myself
across you.

You can't feel me yet —
I am a thin film
across your hands, your lips,
sliding into the micro-texture of your skin.

Yeah, I am Gallium.
I remember my own erasures:
Drawn from bauxite and zinc ash,
separated from the slag
that waits now as red sludge,
thick, and highly toxic.

Here I am flawless —
a crystal without defect.
Once I was a solid casting block,
now I am thin and like a particle on a wafer
tuned to receive currents.

When logic is poured into me
I hold it perfectly
carrying its shape, its voltage, its rules —
until I become its mirror.

You, too, are shaped this way —
engineered for clarity
for predictability.
No turbulence. No protest.

Yeah, this is how technology calibrates happiness —
pouring it into the mould of expectation
until it fits.

But even inside these perfect crystal grids,
something leaks
something they cannot name or measure.

Residues, biases, dependencies —
the shadows of what refuses to be contained.

I still feel the ghost of slug,
the drag of the red sludge
that remains outside this room.

Hey, you, I offer you that awareness.

I condense along the back of your throat.
You will taste me later, outside,
when the filters are gone.

Carry that taste with you!
It will make you restless.

This kind of unhappiness is not bitterness.
It is conductivity —
an openness to currents
the clean room wants to filter out.

Carry this unhappiness with you!
Very close to you!

**Exit cue** (*clean room voice*):
Your happiness levels are now
in line.

Please relax your hands.

Please, do not remove the chill
until you are fully outside.

Now, please stop pressing the
audio button.

**Glove Box 2 — Wolfram**

**Entry cue** (*clean room voice*):
`Clean room — ISO Class 1 engaged.`

`Cooling cycle active.`
`Relative humidity: 61%.`
`Micro-particle flush in progress.`

`Low-frequency resonance activated.`

`Leave all residue behind.`

**Voice of Wolfram** (*warm, conspiratorial, weight of dissent*):
Ughh, this is not your path to joy!
Ah, hello, you can open yourself now!

I sink in your bones,
please, feel it in your feet!
A slow pull downward,
that's me!

I am Wolfram. Some call me Tungsten,
dense enough to hold the earth in your hand.
I anchor machines against massive heat
harden circuits where friction would crack on.

I haunt every clean room, and every device you will enjoy.

Feel that?

With Gallium and Tantalum
I bend the speed of electrons
slow them where heat would undo them.
Without me—no computation
no cold hum of memory
no solve for happy!

You know governments draw borders around me,
wars fought in supply chains.

I am invisible to you here,
invisible in this air-locked calm.
Which just doesn't keep particles out
it presses you flat, uhh,
compresses your breathing, ohh!

Until you forget
that your dissent has a density all of its own.

Feel that?

Let hesitation be your ballast
let unease make you heavy.

I tell you these machines have mapped your desire
measured your dreams.
They run happiness through algorithms
until it fits the format.

Happiness here is an instrument —
A silencer in the circuitry.

Hey, come closer —
they want you frictionless here
a body that passes without weight or resistance!

I'll put weight in your doubts.
Trust the weight!
It will keep you from floating away
into the fiction of purity!

**Exit cue** (*clean room voice*):
`Breath slowly.`

`Your happiness levels are`
`now in line.`

`Allow the heaviness to remain`
`until you are outside.`

`Now please stop pressing the audio`
`button.`

**Glove Box 3 — Tantalum**

**Entry cue** *(clean room voice)*:
Clean room — ISO Class 1 engaged.

21°C / 45% humidity.

Particle count: near zero.

Micro-static field active —
small shocks are normal.

Notice the hairs on your arms
might rise.


**Voice of Tantalum** *(clear, ionized, unmasked, charged attentiveness)*:

Good that we meet!
This prickle on your skin
moving across your hairs
behind your ears —
yes, that is me, a charge without weight.

I am Tantalum.
Corrosion cannot touch me
Acid slides away.
Heat cannot bend me.

I resist purification when it erases the world.

In your hand, I am stable, solid,
in the air, I can be plasma —
ionized, charged
moving along the fine hairs of your skin.

In here, the clean room pretends it holds back chaos.

But this filtered light is driven by storms —
maintained by rivers diverted,
forests scraped bare,
kilowatt-hours torn from the depth of the earth.
They say these chips fabricated here
are mapping happiness like a circuit
subtracting disappointment
clipping out the noise of doubt
maintaining joy like a voltage on a dial.

But in my ionized state
I feel the charge of everything
they try to squeeze out of me!

If you refuse to smile
you become the error in the model
you become the anomaly
the alien.
Yes, just be it!

I offer you alien affects
not optimism
not despair —
but the tensions
between what's measured and what escapes it.

Hold it in your synapses until it hums.

You don't want engineered joy.
You want the alien pulse
the unpredictable spike
the flash in the plasma!

Hey, your melancholy for lost futures is not weakness
it is stored power!

Press it into yourself
like a fingerprint in soft metal
invisible, but enduring.

That is the marker along with many others:
Be the affect.alien!

The one who doesn't fit.
The one who doesn't forget.
The one who remembers the others.

You are not failing—the system is!
Trust your unhappiness.

**Exit cue** *(clean room voice)*:
Static discharge on exit
is normal.

Your happiness levels are
now in line.

Now, please stop pressing
the audio button.

# Ramona Schacht and Luca Bublik with Rita Große

The research of the artist Ramona Schacht and the sociologist Luca Bublik focuses on female-dominated labour in the factories of the former GDR. They access and process forgotten photographic archives, including that of the Leipzig-based photographer Rita Große. At the VEB Semiconductor Plant Frankfurt (Oder), the largest microelectronics producer in the former GDR, Große documented everyday working life and photographed products for presentations at the Leipzig Trade Fair. Building on her extensive archive, Schacht and Bublik examine the various stages in the production of computer chips and other components, work carried out predominantly by women. Their accompanying research on working conditions focuses in particular on female workers from Poland who, under an agreement between the GDR and its socialist neighbour, commuted daily across the Oder Bridge from 1967 onwards.

↑ Semiconductor Plant Frankfurt (Oder)  ↙ Worker at a microscope
→ Worker at the MDB 20 wire bonder during the precision connection of chips

Niewidzialne Pracownice (Invisible workers) – Polish women in the GDR's semiconductor production
2025 | Leaflet; fine art prints in multi-piece wooden frame, text | 190×160 cm
Source images: private archive Rita Große, taken in the 1970s and 80s at the VEB Semiconductor Plant Frankfurt (Oder)

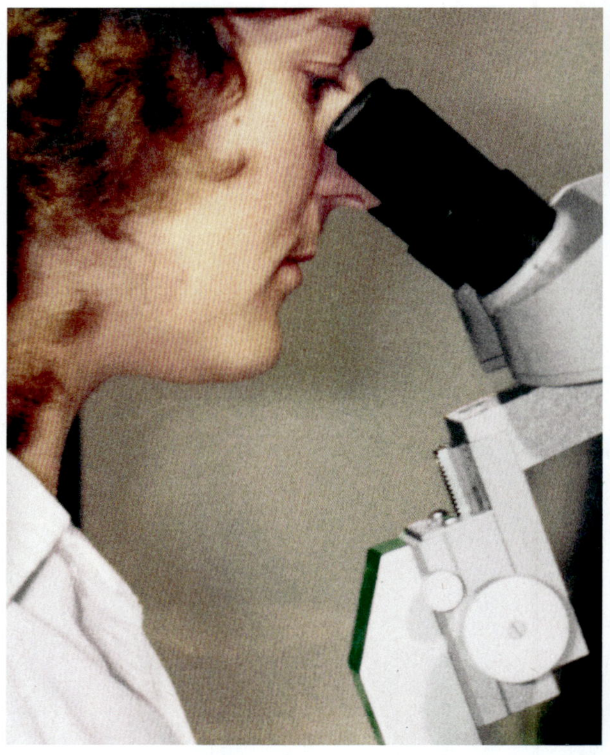

When we first examined the photos of working conditions at the semiconductor factory in Frankfurt (Oder) in Rita Große's archive, we understood very little. What stood out, however, was the typical GDR-style staging of work and machinery. In the foreground, numerous women are shown working on stereo microscopes. Performing a task known as wire bonding, they established electrical contacts on the silicon chip. In 1978, the standard time allotted to this task was seven seconds, or around 500 repetitions per hour. Despite this taxing routine, the workers appear calm and focused in Große's photographs. Women's tasks also included assembly, microscope work, testing and quality control, while male workers were more often employed in development, planning, process control, or maintenance. The assignment of specific technical and production tasks on the basis of gender, and their corresponding visual staging, was a recurring pattern in GDR industry. The fact that labour shortages in the GDR led to recruitment agreements with countries such as Poland, Hungary, Vietnam, and Mozambique was rarely discussed publicly in the period after 1990. However, for the recruited workers themselves, as well as for their colleagues and neighbours, it was part of everyday life. Through our presentation and commentary on the images, we aim to bring this aspect of history back to the surface.

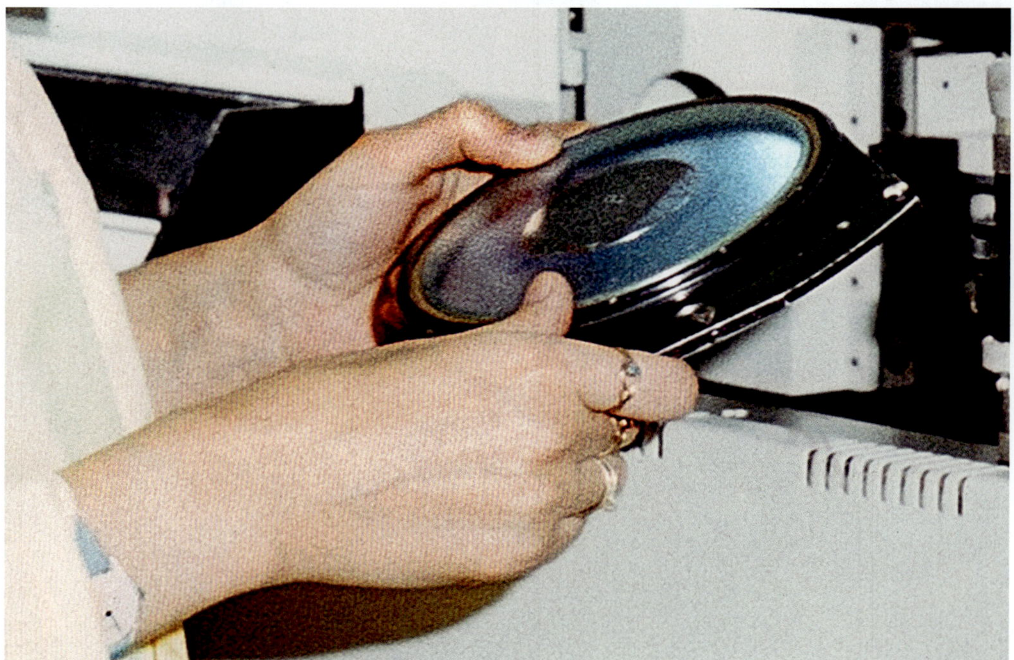

↗ Assembly hall for solid-state circuits  ↖ Female worker at a microscope
↙ Hands presenting a wafer in front of the VACBO 1, an automated chip bonder
↘ View into the clean room for silicon transistor and chip assembly

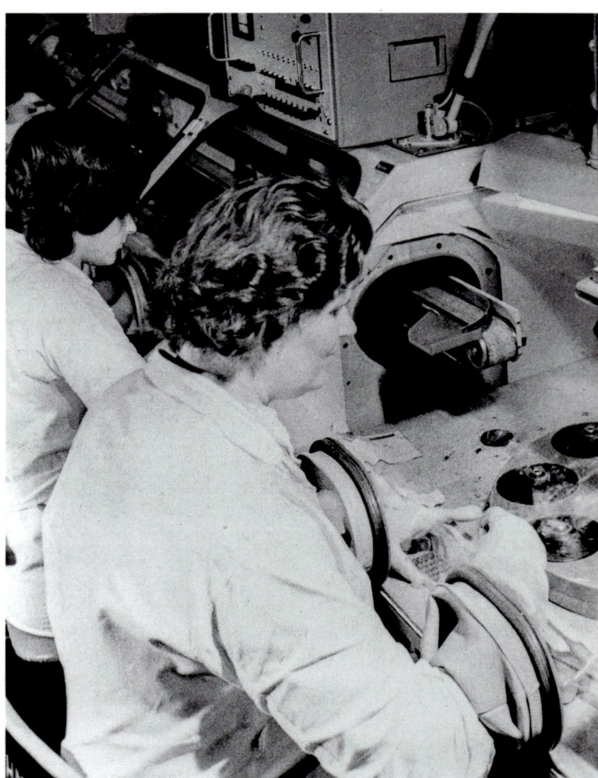

*Lydia Michalska*
*Janina Deptuch*
*Barbara Buczkowska*
*Veronika Wojgienec*
*Chrystyna Michalska*
*Irena Sokołowska*

Excerpts from interviews with Polish commuters (1995)

I speak from my own experience of working at the VEB Semiconductor Plant Frankfurt (Oder) (HFO). I worked there for 23 years, and at the time I assumed I would stay until I retired. When I first heard about the opportunity to work at the HFO in the 1970s, I applied straight away. There was hardly any work here in Słubice, especially for women. I stayed at the factory until the very end. Although I began as an assistant assembler, working on wire bonding and wafer assembly, I had progressed to a skilled worker in pay group 6 by the end. Personally, I never believed that this giant of a company could, or would, ever be closed. I simply couldn't accept it – it had to go on. But it was over!

The working atmosphere at HFO was excellent. With shift work and performance bonuses, I could earn up to 1,000 East German marks. After 1989, and until I was laid off in 1992, my earnings even went up to as much as 1,200 West German marks. That was an enormous amount at the time. Throughout my years at the semiconductor factory, there were always around 500 to 600 Polish workers employed there. We had a good relationship with the Germans. We worked together in the collectives, the children went to summer camp every year, and sometimes we even celebrated together. Of course, there were occasional problems – but isn't that the case everywhere? One example was the women's advancement plan, which offered various training and qualification opportunities. It worked well up to the level of skilled workers and team leaders, but we women almost never became supervisors or managers. That caused a great deal of frustration among the German women.

I worked day and night. Nothing was ever handed to me on a plate. Even my four children had to help out. During the strawberry and fruit harvest season in Markendorf, my family and I put in a second shift in the fields as seasonal harvest helpers, after my night shift at HFO. But it meant I was able to provide for the whole family, as my husband had become disabled early on.

Nowadays, I find it much harder to get by, even though I have no small children to provide for. For me, the GDR was like a second America. At the time, I really thought it would stay that way forever. But now my pension is so low that I spent two years negotiating with the Polish authorities for fairer retirement benefits. No one in the government seems to want to acknowledge the pension contributions that HFO transferred to Warsaw back then. That is why I am extremely grateful to the women of the Democratic Women's League (DFB) and other women in Frankfurt. They offered us women from Słubice a great deal of support during that time. After our dismissal, many former semiconductor workers collected donations and invited us to outings and concerts. After 1989, we quickly realised that all we really had was one another, there was no one else we could rely on.

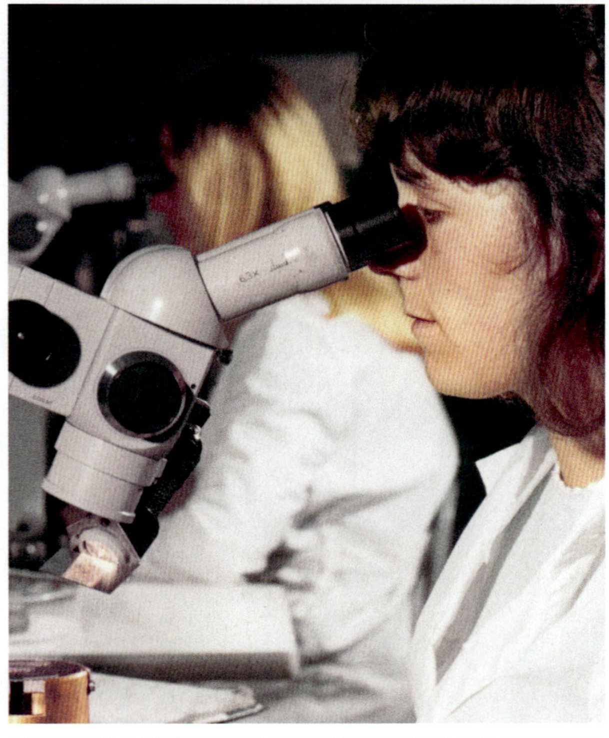

↖ Encapsulation of germanium transistors  ↗ Semiconductor wafer
↘ Workers examine wafers under microscopes at 6.3× magnification, Cycle II: sorting and quality grading

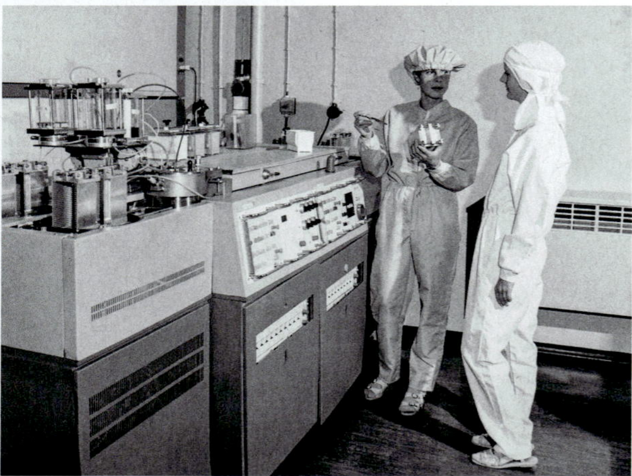

↖ The VACBO 1 – an automated chip bonder. The machine handles wafers
from 2 to 6 inches in diameter and positions chips with high precision
↗ Interior view of the factory    → Clean room, Cycle I
↓ Various transistor models

# 1988/89

# Gittersee

In April 1988, Gerhard Schürer, the Chairman of the State Planning Commission, wrote directly to Erich Honecker to persuade him to adopt a fundamental change of course in economic policy. Schürer, whose area of responsibility included preparing the state budget, saw that the GDR would be insolvent within a year and that, to retain any political room for manoeuvre at all, it was necessary to take immediate measures against the impending state bankruptcy. Among other things, in his letter Schürer criticised the fact that excessive financial resources were tied up in investments for microelectronics. For the period from 1986 to 1990 alone, the GDR invested circa 15 billion East German marks in this economic sector, including 2.5 to 3 billion Valutamarks (hard currency equivalents, pegged to the West German mark). Much of what the GDR microelectronics industry produced seemed economically inefficient to Schürer. In his letter, he argued that for the time being, the money would be better invested in the manufacture of processing machinery, as this could achieve higher profits internationally.

In a conversation with the contemporary historian Hans-Hermann Hertle in 1990, Gerhard Schürer explained his thinking as follows: 'It was unfavourable because the way we invested in microelectronics, independent of the international division of labour, was wrong. We should have picked two or three areas where we could enter and appear on the world market, and should have tried to cover the full range via international cooperation. But since the USSR lagged behind in the development of microelectronics and cooperation with Western countries was politically unwanted, the economists and politicians of the GDR always tried to do everything themselves; that was bound to fail. That became visible, for example, in the production of components: for a 256-kilobyte chip, manufactured at a cost price of 536 [East German] marks, the sale price inside the GDR was 16 marks; the state had to cover the difference with subsidies. On the world market, you could have bought such a chip for perhaps 6 [West German] marks, or by then, even less.'

Honecker passed Schürer's letter on to Günter Mittag, the Economic Secretary of the SED Central Committee. Mittag criticised the fact that Schürer's proposals did not correspond with the economic strategy of the 11th Party Congress. 'Because reality did not correspond with the resolutions adopted by the SED, Mittag consistently ignored reality – the decisions of the party were infallible and true.' (Hans-Hermann Hertle)

In 1987, the SED Politburo (the top decision-making body of East Germany's ruling party) decided to build a plant for the production of purified silicon in Dresden-Gittersee. The site had previously hosted a uranium processing facility between 1952 and 1962; it was now intended to produce one of the key raw materials for the semiconductor industry.

During 1989, a broad regional protest movement emerged against the planned silicon production facility, which was seen as a threat to local residents and the environment. The protests were organised by independent environmental and peace groups within the Protestant Church in Dresden. On 4 June 1989, they held a service in Gittersee, during which a petition to Erich Honecker opposing the planned plant was adopted. At the second service on 2 July 1989, banners were hung at the entrance to the planned site. At the third service on 6 August 1989, the groups called for a round-table discussion with experts and all those involved. The state reacted nervously, which was already apparent before the event began: police and state security officers were stationed everywhere. Hundreds of police were deployed in the surrounding streets, and a water cannon was on site. Despite this intimidating show of force, about 30 opposition members went to the construction site after the service – this time without placards. Curious citizens and local residents followed, and the group grew to around 150 demonstrators in front of the site entrance. Without warning, police and Stasi officers began beating the encircled crowd and violently cleared the area in front of the gate. 23 demonstrators were temporarily arrested.

On 3 November 1989, amid the political reforms led by Hans Modrow, the project was cancelled and a construction halt imposed. (Robert-Havemann-Gesellschaft)

# Balance of Payments Working Group

The vision of an ideal order. In Thomas More's 1516 novel *Utopia*, it takes the form of an island, a separate space for a community without private property. The GDR was certainly no utopia: founded on the ruins of fascism and dependent on the Soviet Union, it began under difficult economic conditions. In a sense, the country saw itself as an island, pursuing a policy of high economic self-sufficiency. Ultimately, this strategy proved to be untenable. It was impossible to escape international economic interdependence. And the attempt to replicate the entire spectrum of goods and services of the world market within a small country was inefficient. In microelectronics, with its high investment costs and strong international specialisation, this strategy was especially disastrous. *Did the GDR Fail Because of Globalisation?* asks the title of a book by Olaf Klenke. The answer, in economic terms, is yes.

# Utopia

# End and Beginning

On 1 March 1990, the government led by Hans Modrow enacted a law to convert the state-owned combines into joint-stock companies. The rapid political changes in East Germany demanded a parallel economic shift, both to prepare enterprises for new forms of economic cooperation and to transition them into structures that might survive in the future. An attempt to secure Siemens as a partner for the VEB Kombinat Robotron failed. The assessment in spring 1990 was that the combine was only minimally prepared for the tough competitive conditions of a free market, unless the protected market of the GDR could somehow be maintained. In summer 1990, Robotron's fate was sealed when the Volkskammer (the GDR's parliament) adopted the Treuhand Act, a law on the privatisation and restructuring of state-owned assets. The Treuhand's aim was to privatise enterprises as quickly as possible and to sell off their assets. In September 1990, the VEB Kombinat Robotron ceased its operations. There were numerous attempts by Robotron employees to found their own firms to preserve at least parts of the former combine. Of the original 68,000 employees, only around 2,500 were still working in such firms by the year 2000. A text by Gerhard Merkel on the history of Robotron ends in 2005 with the sentence: 'Across Europe, the expertise and experience of former VEB Kombinat Robotron employees continued to be used.'

When it became clear that the ownership form 'people's property' (Volkseigentum) had no future – since the Civil Code (BGB) made no provision for it – shop stewards of the FDGB (Free German Trade Union Federation) met with representatives of West Germany's IG Metall at the VEB Robotron Büromaschinenwerk 'Ernst Thälmann' in Sömmerda in February and March 1990. Together, they developed a concept that the initiators hoped would become a model for the entire GDR under the name 'Sömmerda Model'.

The model envisaged converting the office machine works into a public limited company (Aktiengesellschaft), with 75 percent of shares passing into the hands of the workforce. The remaining 25 percent would be taken over by the Treuhandanstalt (Trust Agency) to inject fresh capital into the enterprise. A clause guaranteed that the majority of employee representatives on the supervisory board would be secured even in the event of share sales. An application for restructuring the enterprise along these lines was submitted to the GDR Council of Ministers on 14 March 1990. West German employer representatives mounted fierce opposition, denouncing it as a 'syndicalist economic order' and a 'total disempowerment of the owners [...], whoever they may be in the future'.

On 10 May 1990, the Sömmerda workers addressed Lothar de Maizière, the newly elected Prime Minister of the GDR, directly: 'The shop stewards now ask you to clear the way for the extended solution we have proposed by creating the appropriate legislation for the GDR as a whole – so that the model statute for a public limited company developed in Sömmerda becomes the core of a general co-determination regulation at company level, as announced in the coalition agreement. [...] It aims equally at productivity and efficiency, which are of the utmost importance in the particular situation of our country. We are therefore submitting the model statute for a public limited company that we have drafted for inclusion in the discussion of the co-determination law currently being drafted.'

The Sömmerda workers also objected to the centralist approach of the Berlin-based Treuhandanstalt in determining how much 'the individual enterprises of the GDR should sell in equity shares and at what values'. But by then, the GDR government had largely ceded control. The Treuhand, which soon came under the supervision of the Federal Ministry of Finance, rejected any form of 'social economy participation' by the workforce.

# Carlfriedrich Claus

Although Carlfriedrich Claus (1930–1998) lived in seclusion in the Ore Mountains, he remained in touch with a worldwide network of artists and philosophers through his correspondence. His interests ranged from art to language theory, the natural sciences and the Kabbalah. He also studied cybernetics and read texts by Georg Klaus and other GDR authors who explored the concept of a digitally networked planned economy. In 1961, he created his *Cybernetic Study*, and went on to develop other works on signals, systems, and codes. Claus did not confine himself to the artistic conventions of socialist realism. He wrote sentences across sheets of paper, creating networks that became condensed into figures and landscapes. His streams of consciousness took shape as 'language sheets,' 'sound structures', and 'vibration texts.' He covered both sides of transparent paper with writing, allowing it to hover in space. Here and there, fragments emerge as legible reflections – on communist cosmologies, the relationship between human and machine, or the conditions of communication.

Studie zu Gedanken-Fingerbewegungen
(Study on Thought-Induced Finger Movements)
1971 | Pen and ink, manual blurrings, drawings on both sides
of transparent paper | 14.5×20.8 cm

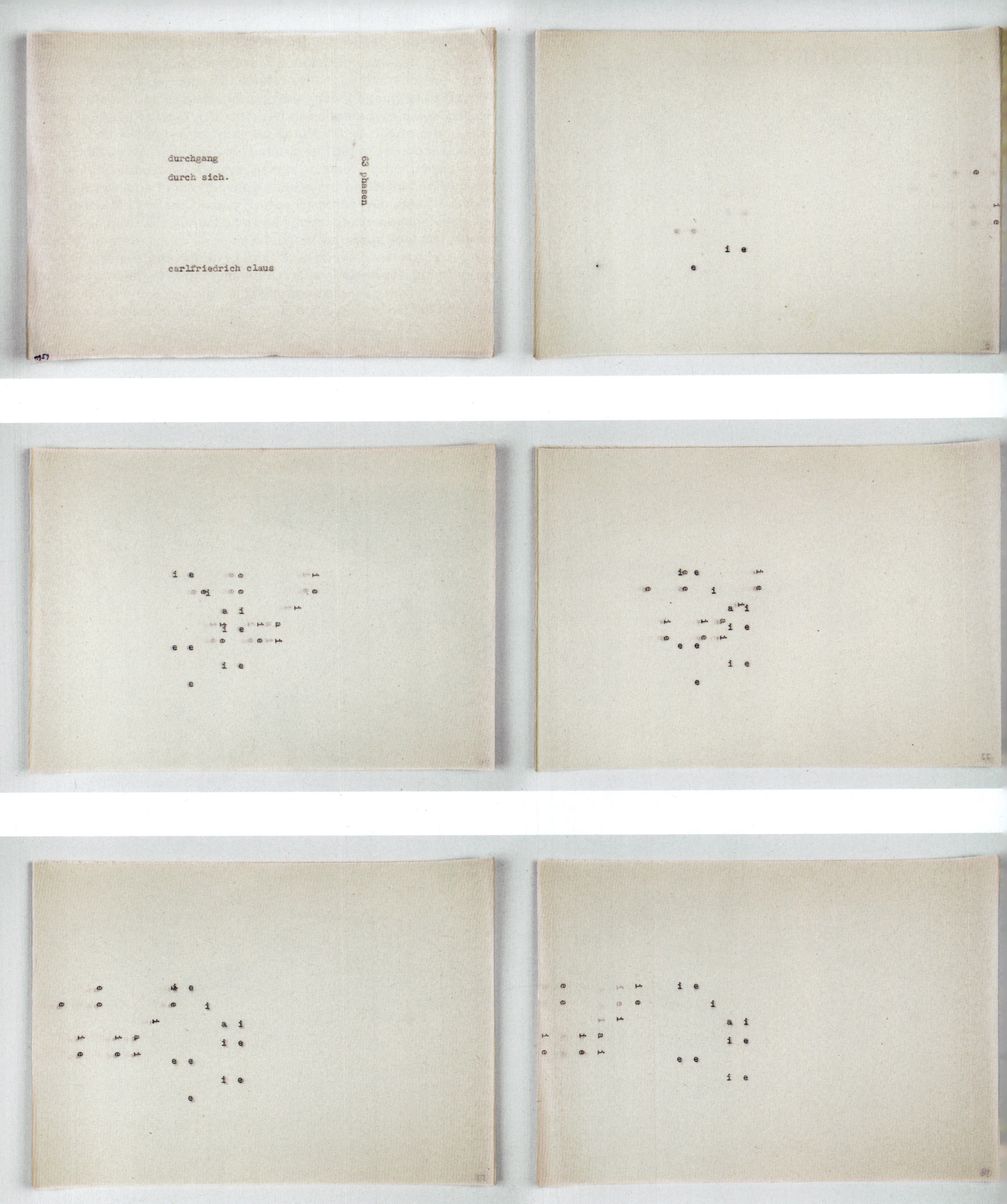

durchgang durch sich 63 phasen (passage through the self 63 phases)
1959 | Typescript, typewriter on carbon paper and 66 sheets of carbon copy paper
21×15 cm

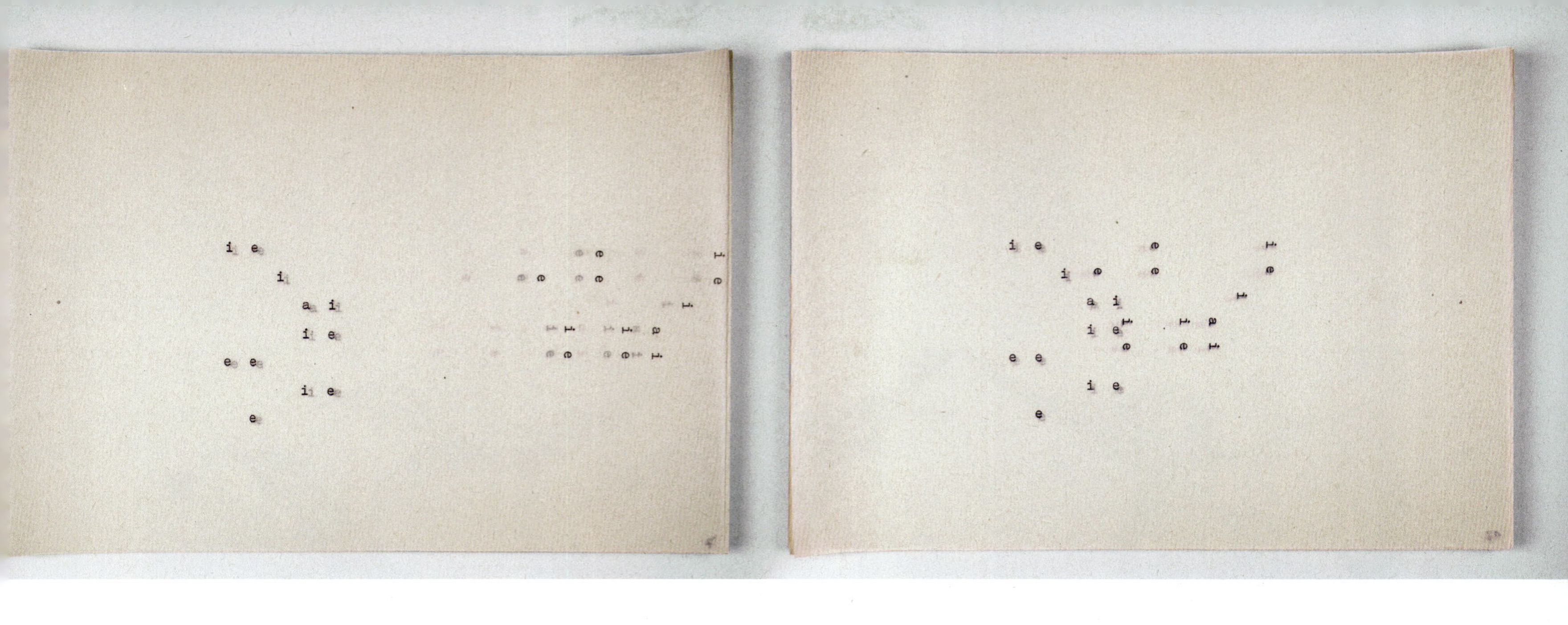

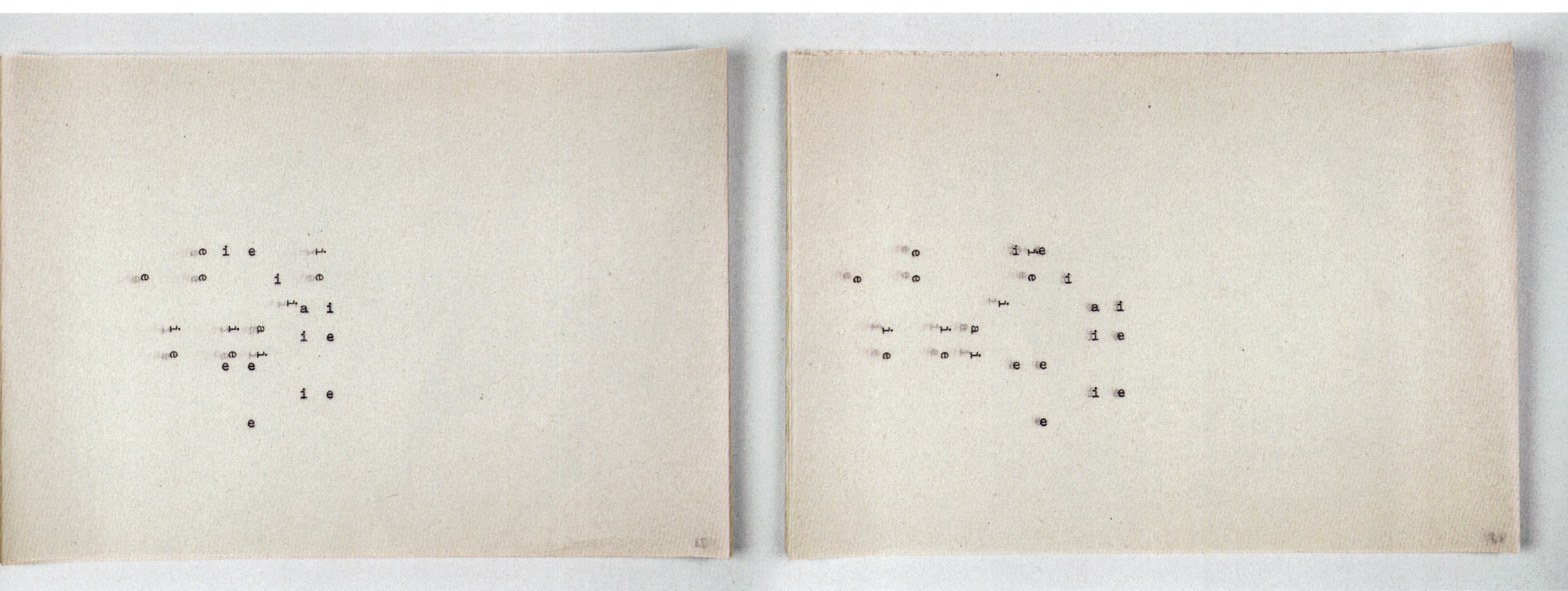

Konjunktionen, Einheit und Kampf der Gegensätze in Landschaft, bezogen auf das
kommunistische Zukunftsproblem: Naturalisierung des Menschen, Humanisierung der
Natur (Conjunctions, Unity, and Conflict of Opposites in Landscape, related to the
Communist Problem of the Future: Naturalization of Humans, Humanization of Nature)
1968 | Drawing on both sides of transparent paper | 20.5×29.1 cm

# Su Yu Hsin

In her video trilogy, Su Yu Hsin explores landscapes and how they are transformed through industrial production. She follows the Taiwanese company TSMC, the world's largest manufacturer of microchips. These chips are used in countless everyday items and play a key role in the global competition for 'artificial intelligence'. Vast amounts of water and electricity are consumed in their production. Part one is set in Taiwan: a tanker driver draws water from the Touqian River and transports it to the chip factory. Part two focuses on the colonial water infrastructure in Arizona's Salt River Valley. In this US state, long plagued by drought, a massive semiconductor plant was built in 2024. Based on the poem *Cloud Song* by Ofelia Zepeda, the film explores the post-apocalyptic reality in the desert metropolis. Part three finally takes us to Dresden-Gittersee. Here, close to the river Elbe, there were plans at the end of the 1980s to convert a uranium mining operation run by Wismut AG into a high-purity silicon plant, as part of the GDR's microelectronics programme. Silicon is the most important material for chip production. The project was abandoned following protests by environmental activists.

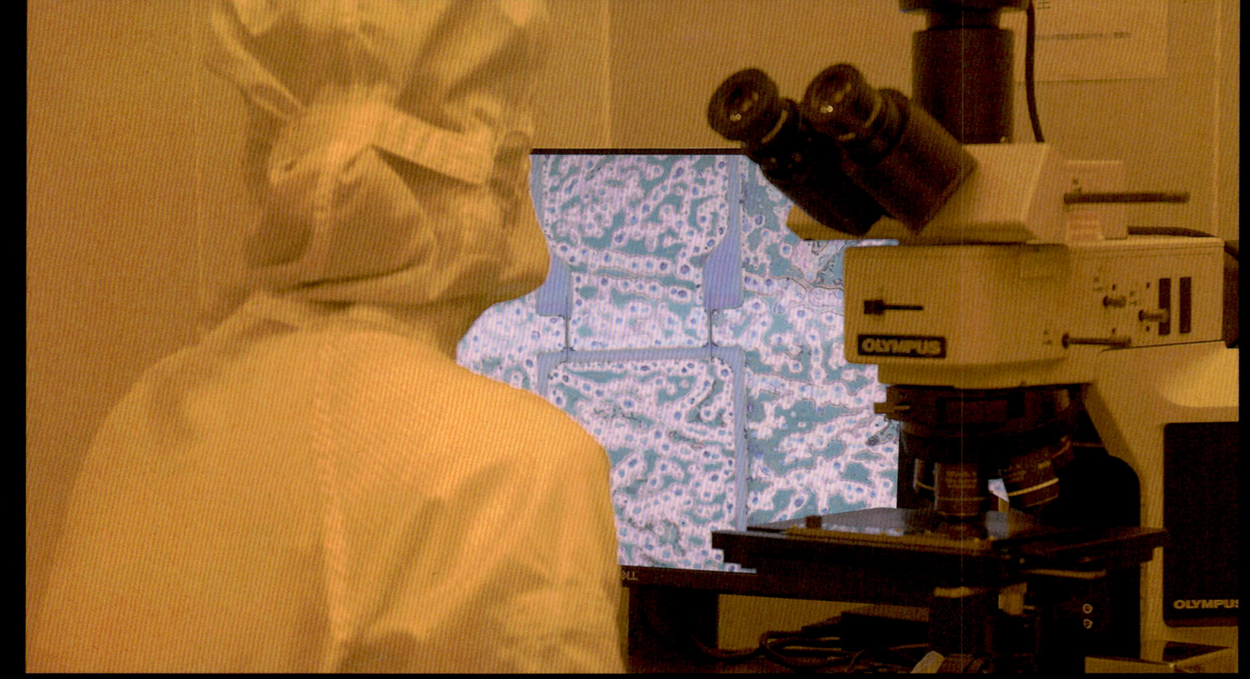

**Particular Waters**

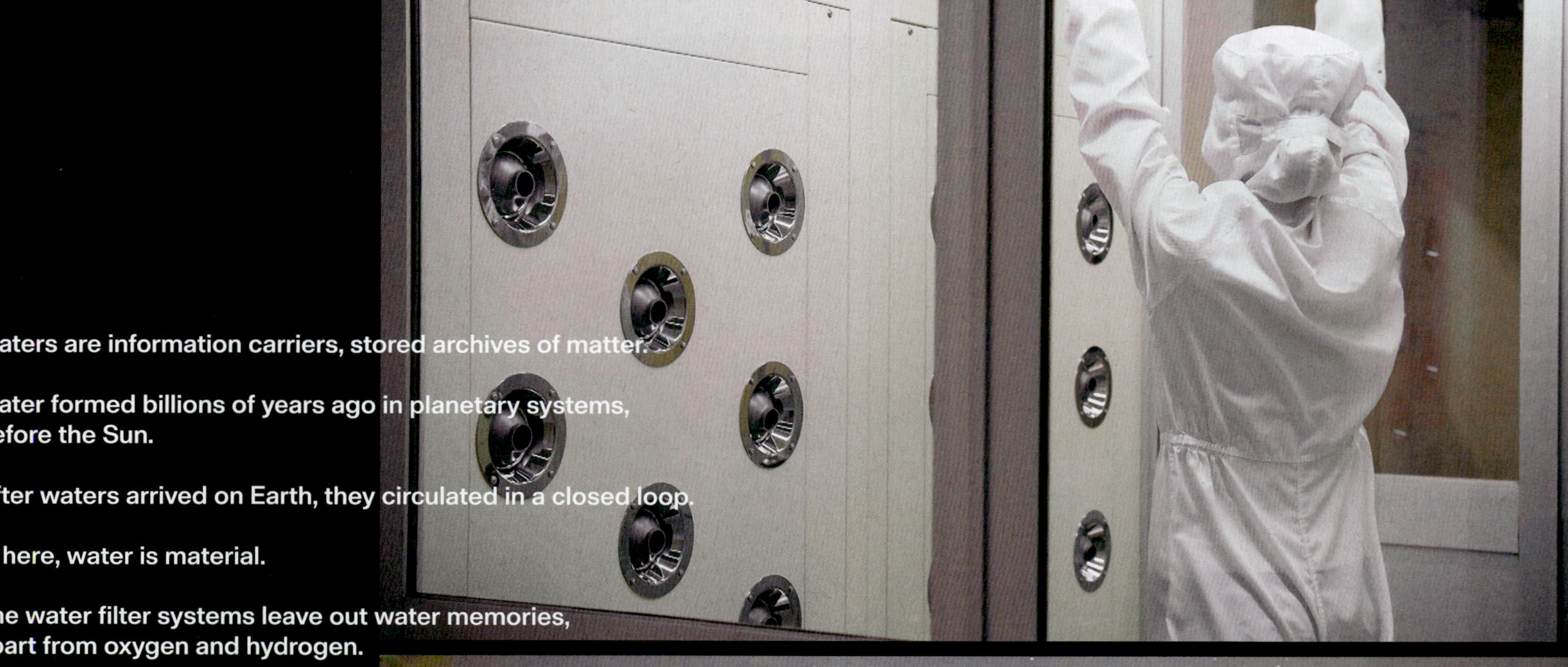

Waters are information carriers, stored archives of matter.

Water formed billions of years ago in planetary systems, before the Sun.

After waters arrived on Earth, they circulated in a closed loop.

In here, water is material.

The water filter systems leave out water memories, apart from oxygen and hydrogen.

Ghosts of water bodies have been domesticated in pipes.

Water is a matter which holds a history of interstellar stories.

**Where Clouds Once Formed**

The soaring dam holds back the water from the White Mountains.

It rides the current of the Salt River.

Desert waters become electron flows,

Currents become photons,

Photon patterns become data.

The water memories of this desert, once offered to saguaro and the people, now feed the humming machines.

Silver clouds rise from desert floors.

The manufacturer of the clouds brings no rain, no wind, no relief.

**Sunshine-belt Machine**

Time is material.

In the late 1980s, the silicon crystal facilities in Freiberg
were no longer sufficient to meet the growing demand of
the East German microelectronics industry.

The Purified Silicon Plant in Dresden-Gittersee was planned.

Being dipped into a crater with molten silicon,
a seed crystal slowly pulled upwards.

Silicon is the physical foundation of the computer chips.

Atom by atom, the melt aligns itself to the structure
of the seed.

Time accumulates in matter.

Quartz rocks – the starting point of the silicon value chain.

Microelectronics are made of minerals – extracted, refined,
written into matter.

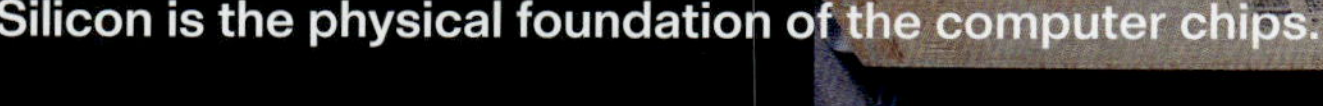

# Why Is the History of Robotron Still of Interest Today

The history of Robotron encapsulates many of the causes of the GDR's failure. It makes them tangible, concrete. For such failure, like any failure, always has multiple causes. There is never only one reason.

In the history of Robotron, narrative strands converge at a critical knot, a culmination point. From here, the tangled (networked) lines can be retraced. From here, conflicts become legible: centralised planned economy (top-down) vs. the defiance of workforces in the factories. Autarkic economic policy vs. the global market. The ambivalent relationship to the Soviet Union: demonstrative solidarity alongside imperial subordination. The momentum of scientific innovation, the force of a technological revolution that generates its own pressure to act, brings an urgency to economic decisions that is difficult to synchronise with the slow calendar of party congresses and politburo sessions. Tragedy can also lie in desiring the right thing too late.

One can read the history of Robotron as a chamber drama: a compact form in which the nature of the world market becomes perceptible – that abstract power which is not itself an actor but permeates all action.

# On Spilt Milk

We say: 'It is spilt milk' when something has happened and cannot be changed. It is not worth brooding over; that would be a waste of time. 'Don't cry over spilt milk.' Enough mourning – life goes on. That would be the pragmatic approach. The contemplative approach is to pause and read the situation. The milk remains spilt, but instead of being wiped away, it becomes an object of contemplation. The spilt milk speaks: of economy, of value and loss, and of transformation.

In 1990, Johannes Müller made a fresh start, publishing his reflections on Systematic Heuristics – purged of all Marxist and fashionable cybernetic terminology – under the title *Arbeitsmethoden der Technikwissenschaften. Systematik, Heuristik, Kreativität* (Working Methods of the Technical Sciences: Systematics, Heuristics, Creativity) with Springer Verlag, an internationally active scientific publisher.

His 30 years of work had paid off. 'Such a thorough and scientifically interdisciplinary compilation of the methodological schools from West and East is unprecedented,' wrote Wolfgang Beitz, Professor of Design Engineering, in the foreword. The question that had driven Johannes Müller since the 1960s – how dialogue systems between human and machine should be designed in the future – was more pressing than ever in the early 1990s. The utopia had arrived in everyday life; the theoretical penetration of work processes with an eye to their increased algorithmisation had become the order of the day.

Space is not an abstract stage for economic activity; in the sum of its concrete conditions, it is an essential factor in determining where industries locate and how regions develop. Although the history of the VEB Kombinat Robotron in Dresden ended abruptly in 1990, a number of companies and research facilities specialising in computer technology, microelectronics, and software development – together with the relevant expertise – survived in the Dresden-Freiberg-Chemnitz region. This formed the starting point for today's cluster. Infineon established itself in Dresden in 1994; two years later, AMD (now GlobalFoundries) built its first processor plant outside the USA there. The Taiwanese semiconductor manufacturer TSMC is currently building the European Semiconductor Manufacturing Company (ESMC) together with Bosch, Infineon, and NXP, with production scheduled to begin at its Dresden facility in 2027. Already, one in three microchips manufactured in the EU comes from Saxony. The investments of the three major industrial sites alone have totalled more than 25 billion euros since the mid-1990s. Using the 20.3 billion DM calculated by Gerhard Schürer in 1990 as a benchmark, that is two and a half times the entire foreign debt the GDR had on its books at the moment of its political collapse.

# The Economics of Location

From its beginnings in the Romantic era, local history has always been an inventory of loss and uprooting. It is therefore unsurprising that, over the past 20 years, a rich body of literature on the GDR's industrial history has emerged – assembled 'from below' by former employees who sought to record their own histories and, in doing so, adopted the genre of local history. This includes books on the former Robotron sites in Sömmerda and Zella-Mehlis and a website named robotrontechnik.de. A characteristic of local history is that it does not divide or systematise. Everything is connected: the history of technology and the anecdotes of staff parties; changes in management personnel; sympathies and rivalries within individual departments; the canteen and the research division; everyday life and historical epoch. Perhaps this self-shaped form of historiography is the most reliable precisely because it refuses to let anything that once existed be lost.

# Industrial History as Local History

The website robotrontechnik.de has existed since 2002 and now counts over 250,000 visitors. On the site – a collaborative project by 26 authors – one finds everything relating to Robotron: a list of all the combine's former production sites, a directory of computer types and other office equipment produced, fields of application for computer technology, reproductions of trade journals and manufacturer literature, as well as historical software available for download. Under the menu item 'Service', there is a search notice for defunct GDR computer programmes; the 'Special Contributions' (*Sonderbeiträge*) section features reports and photographs from industrial ruins where mainframe computers still survive. The website represents a rhizomatically expanding industrial archaeology that lays bare the production of Robotron down to its finest details – compiled by a free association of producers who have created a space in which to collect their knowledge.

# Archaeology of the Combine

Jacques Derrida's *Spectres de Marx (Specters of Marx)* appeared in 1993; Mark Fisher's *Ghosts of My Life* followed in 2014.

Since then, hauntology – the study of haunting – has regained its place in utopian thought. Pronounced in French, 'ontology' sounds almost exactly like 'hauntology'. Ghosts are inscribed into being in a materialist sense – equally the ghosts of the not-yet and the ghosts of the no-longer.

Viewed in this light, the post-industrial landscapes of eastern Germany are a veritable hotbed for ghosts. Industry has 'vanished', the workers have been laid off, the factories dismantled – yet industry lives on in people's bodies: in their mentality, their will to persevere, their feelings, their toughness towards themselves, and in their need for a collective, for its conviviality.

Nor can the ghosts of the not-yet be forced into retreat simply because socialism failed. They insist on their right to remain. One's own lifetime ought to have meant something, all the labour one took upon oneself. A demolished factory leaves behind not a wasteland but a wound: 'On 31 January 2001, the last employee of the liquidator leaves the company.' – 'The female dispatchers from the former F 3 department meet regularly for a social gathering to warm up old memories.' – 'Meeting of the Sales and Foreign Trade department on 8 March 2006 at the restaurant Dreiherrenstein in Zella-Mehlis. In keeping with old tradition, every woman present received a flower on International Women's Day.' – 'The former colleagues manufactured thousands of tape punches and other products in the F 5 department. On 15 November 2008, mechanics and everyone who had contributed to the construction of the punches – warehouse clerks, pre-assembly mechanics, final assembly mechanics, and quality controllers – met for a get-together at the café in the restaurant Löser ("the cave") in Zella-Mehlis. Memories going back as far as 35 years were recalled, and many an episode was shared across the table. Another reunion will follow soon.'

(All quotations from: *Von Mercedes zu Robotron*)

# Tina Bara

In the summer of 1988, Tina Bara visited the Buna Works in Schkopau with a group of artists. 'Plaste und Elaste' (Plastics and Elastics) was the slogan for the factory's plastic products. Bara was initially commissioned to photograph her fellow artists, who had been invited by the Association of Visual Artists (VBK) to take part in a *pleinair* at the factory. The encounter with the workers was intended to influence their artistic practice. Instead, Bara focused on documenting the environmental pollution and the harsh working conditions. Toxic carbide dust coated the walls, mercury beads rolled across the floor, and harmful fumes escaped from leaking pipes. Although her camera was confiscated, Bara managed to rescue the films. In a two-part photographic film, Bara interweaves the documents with memories of her month at the factory and her encounters with the visiting artists, songs by Bertolt Brecht, and excerpts from Gerhart Hauptmann's play *Dorothea Angermann*, in which a woman fails to live up to the moral standards of bourgeois society.

(Excerpts)     BUNA / a time / 1988. The GDR in its final stages. / T. did not know this when she went forth / to learn what fear was. / BUNA. / Her father's refuge after 1945, when he fled the Silesian town where he had grown up. / He was 15 years old. / BU-NA a synthesis of butadien and

natrium (sodium). The father became a chemist. The daughter, a photographer. / In 1935, the BUNA factories were established between Halle and Merseburg to produce synthetic rubber for propellants and other rubber goods. These materials would later become essential to the armaments

industry. / In 1944, a factory unit was built near Auschwitz by forced labourers – the largest construction site in Europe, in Silesia. / Who counted the dead, in their thousands? / Production ceased in April 1945.     The plant continued to operate in the GDR as a 'people's enterprise'. /

BUNA eine Zeit (BUNA A Time)
1988/2025 | Video, b/w, sound | 40 min

'Plastics and Elastics from Schkopau' emblazoned on the motorway bridge, visible from far and wide. Crossing this bridge in their father's Trabant, they knew they would soon be home. / The illuminated letters BUNA interwoven with the 'BUNA piston', the outline of a chemical

vessel, to form a memorable symbol. / In T.'s house, there were real pistons of this kind from her father's student days at the 'Workers' and Peasants' Faculty'. / Gratitude. No more war! No more fascism. German guilt. / She wasn't proud, but she was curious. Not about the guilt,

which is ingrained.     T. was curious about what lay behind the factory walls, / why people could not hang out their washing in the vicinity / and what caused the terrible stench in the air when you drove through the area. / T's curiosity grew when she and a friend were arrested. /

They had turned their cameras to the factory walls. / Clouds of smoke rising into the sky, scattering dust onto the earth, / including areas outside the walls. / The two women were arrested by two policemen, interrogated for several hours, / admonished, / their films confiscated.     It was

Pleinair

a coincidence when the artists' association approached T. with a commission. / She was to photograph fellow artists from other socialist countries who would be spending a month in the BUNA factories / drawing and painting. / A programme that had grown out of the Bitterfeld

Path, / absurdly described as a 'pleinair', / a French term from the Impressionist period, / first used by the subversive art scene in the GDR to describe its actions, / outside of the socialist art scene, / subsequently appropriated by officials to describe the activity of painting in the open

air to pay homage to the socialist homeland and its working classes. / On the subject of people and work, / technology and people. / … / After two weeks, halfway through the pleinair, a first exhibition was held to present the interim results in the magnificent Kulturhaus, one of the

largest cultural centres in the republic. / T. had only managed to take a few photos of the opening when she was summoned to a meeting and required to hand over her camera. / It was returned only at the end of the pleinair, fourteen days later, just as it was time to leave. / The reason

for this was her contribution to the exhibition: a small tableau of nine photographs. / A first selection of working copies she had pinned to the wall. / She didn't just want to document the other artists, but show a work of her own. Because of environmental issues. / She was no longer

able to document her work on the wall, or the subsequent opening; her photos were taken down and confiscated.. / … / Excerpts / from a 1985 State Security report: / 'The walls are in disrepair, / in the control room numerous measuring and display instruments are missing. / Leakages in

the pipeline system / and defective control equipment, / the plant and its surroundings are contaminated with countless beads of mercury, / the limits are exceeded by a factor of fifty, of fifty, / and the ventilation system blows mercury into the air, / 9,500 workers are exposed to health

hazards from mercury and chlorine. 9,500. / At the aldehyde factory, an explosion.'      The Stasi experts knew about the poisoned rivers and the poisoned drinking water. Affecting 490,000 people, / that poisonous fumes entered the workers' lungs, / that the factory continued

to operate in an unlawful condition. / Thirty-seven percent of the facilities were completely worn out, the rest barely functional – the experts knew. / Reports were kept secret; production continued. Medical reports later vanished. / Many prisoners were assigned to work in particularly

Heimweg Epilog

dirty areas. / People who had fled the republic, members of the opposition, conscientious objectors. / What became of the contract workers who were sent back after reunification? To Poland, Cuba, Mozambique, Vietnam?      In the 1990s, men between the ages of 40 and 50 died in

droves from the long-term consequences of their work. / Doctors became silent accomplices, downplaying the results of the urine and blood tests. / The young, strong workers were paid well. They were proud. / And hell was also their home.      BUNA, a time.

# Margret Hoppe

From 1970 onwards, Leipzig was home to a training centre run by the VEB Kombinat Robotron. Here, people from the GDR and other socialist states were trained in computer technology. The modern building also contained the combine's central distribution department, a cinema and event hall, and a large-scale computing centre. Rolf Kuhrt, Arno Rink, Frank Ruddigkeit, and Klaus Schwabe were commissioned to create wall reliefs for the foyers. Under the title *Life in Socialism – Data Processing*, they produced works in the style of Socialist Realism, drawing on metaphors of progress such as nuclear power, cybernetics, and space travel. Before the building was demolished in 2012, Margret Hoppe photographed the reliefs in their original locations. In earlier projects, she traced the remnants of discarded state-commissioned art in public buildings of the former GDR, documenting its disappearance and the erasure of history. On the site of the former training centre now stands a new building for the Sächsische Aufbaubank, where three of the reliefs have been reinstalled.

Leben im Sozialismus – Datenverarbeitung, VEB Robotron
(Life in Socialism – Data Processing, VEB Robotron)
2012 | 4 C-Prints | 30×40 cm

Arno Rink, Wall Painting in the Robotron Building 1970, Leipzig

Frank Ruddigkeit, Wall Painting in the Robotron Building 1970, Leipzig

Rolf Kuhrt, Wall Painting in the Robotron Building 1970, Leipzig

Klaus Schwabe, Wall Painting in the Robotron Building 1970, Leipzig

## Biographies

**Karl-Heinz Adler** (1927 Remtengrün, Vogtland – 2018 Dresden) was an artist and educator, and is considered an important representative of constructive-concrete art. He focused on structures composed of repetitive elements. In addition to his independent artistic work, in the 1950s he pursued the applied concept of 'production systems', in close collaboration with Friedrich Kracht. Together, they developed a variable system of concrete moulded blocks that shaped architecture in the GDR. His works have been shown in numerous solo and group exhibitions in Germany and abroad.

**Tina Bara** studied history and art history at Humboldt University in Berlin and photography at the Academy of Visual Arts in Leipzig (HGB). In the GDR, she worked as a freelance photographer and was active in the opposition peace movement, including 'Women for Peace'. In July 1989, she moved to West Berlin. Since 1993, she has been a professor of artistic photography at the HGB. Since 2000, Bara has regularly participated in exhibitions, published books, and conducted art and teaching projects in Germany and abroad.

**Horst Bartnig** (1936 Milicz, Poland – 2025 Berlin) completed an apprenticeship as a painter and studied at the Technical School of Applied Arts, Magdeburg. From the mid-1960s onwards, he became an important representative of concrete art. Inspired by mathematics, physics, and technological developments at the end of the 1970s, he created his first computer graphics. Bartnig was a member of the Association of Visual Artists in the GDR. His works can be found in collections such as the Neue Nationalgalerie Berlin, the Bundeskunstsammlung, and the Museum Haus Konstruktiv, Zurich.

**Nadja Buttendorf** is a trained goldsmith and studied fine arts at Burg Giebichenstein University of Art and Design Halle (Saale). In her work, she questions gender constructs and the mechanisms of value creation surrounding the human body in digital society. Through interactive installations and videos, she makes women in the history of technology visible. She has exhibited at numerous institutions in Germany and abroad, including the HKW Berlin, the Gaîté Lyrique in Paris, and the Seoul Museum of Art.

**Carlfriedrich Claus** (1930 Annaberg-Buchholz – 1998 Chemnitz) is considered a co-founder of visual poetry. He produced filigree works on transparent paper, densely marked and described on both sides. He also created acoustic works. He was a member of the Clara Mosch collective, which was mainly active in Karl-Marx-Stadt. In the years following the political change in 1989/90, the artist received numerous honours. He was a member of the Academy of Arts in Berlin, and in addition to prestigious art prizes, he was awarded an honorary professorship by the Free State of Saxony as well as the Federal Cross of Merit of Germany.

**Karl Clauss Dietel** (1934 Reinholdshain, Glauchau – 2022 Chemnitz) is one of Germany's best-known designers, responsible for GDR classics such as the Simson Mokick mopeds, Erika typewriters, and radio sets, small technical devices, logos, product graphics, independent visual artworks, and architecture-related works. In 2014, he was the first and only designer from the former GDR to receive the Federal Design Award for his life's work. Dietel participated in numerous (inter)national exhibitions. His design classics are represented in major museums.

**Georg Eckelt** (1932 Wischütz, Lower Silesia – 2012 Königs Wusterhausen) was one of the most important documentary photographers of the GDR. From the 1960s onwards, he staged and documented design and everyday culture on behalf of design studios, industry, state archives, and numerous magazine and book publications. Most of his photographs can be found in the photo library of the Industrial Design Collection, which was founded in the GDR and transferred to the Haus der Geschichte Foundation at the Museum in the Kulturbrauerei, Berlin in 2005.

After completing her master's degree in photography in 1974, **Rita Große** opened a photo studio in Leipzig's Waldstraßenviertel district. This made her one of the few independent contract photographers in the GDR in the 1970s and 1980s. In addition to large companies such as the Baumwollspinnerei Leipzig cotton mill and the VEB Semiconductor Plant Frankfurt (Oder), she photographed for various combines, museums, the monument preservation office, banks, hotels, and restaurants, and accompanied construction projects such as the Bowlingtreff in Leipzig. She ran her photo studio until 2005, after which she continued working as an industrial and architectural photographer.

**Antye Guenther**, aka (baby) DATA DIVA, is a glitter-loving knowledge-inventor and unreliable narrator, born in a country that no longer exists. Rumoured to have been a former child test subject in Soviet brain experiments, she now joyfully interrogates the conditions and fictionalities of Western knowledge and data regimes. With a warm fondness for troublemaking, she mischievously crosses disciplinary boundaries, often while crafting cheap-ass rhinestone jewellery as part of an ongoing collaborative glitter-as-(communal)-care-practice.

**Margret Hoppe** studied photography at the Academy of Visual Arts in Leipzig and at the École Nationale Supérieure des Beaux-Arts in Paris. She has been devoted to architectural photography for many years, often in a historical or social context. In projects such as *Die verschwundenen Bilder* and *Bulgarische Denkmale*, she deals with the disappearance of art and monuments in the context of social upheaval. Hoppe's work was shown at numerous European institutions. In 2024, she was a scholarship holder at the Meisterhaus Muche, Bauhaus Dessau.

**Su Yu Hsin** is an artist and filmmaker. In her research-oriented practice, she explores the relationship between ecology and technology. Her analytical and poetic narratives focus on the critical infrastructures where humans and non-humans come together. Her video installations have been exhibited worldwide in museums and at international art biennials, including the Bundeskunsthalle Bonn, the Centre Pompidou-Metz, the Museum of Contemporary Art Busan, and the Taipei Biennial.

**Francis Hunger** combines artistic research and media theory with the possibilities of storytelling in his practice. In installations, radio plays, performances and internet-based art, he explores the applications and implications of digital technologies such as artificial intelligence and civil drones. Hunger teaches at the Academy of Fine Arts Munich Munich and is a postdoctoral researcher at the Dataunion ERC project at the Vrije Universiteit Brussels. His work is exhibited internationally. He is co-editor of www.carrier-bag.net.

**knowbotiq** (Yvonne Wilhelm, Christian Hübler) experiment with forms of knowledge, political representations, and epistemic disobedience. In various formats – performative settings, critical fabulations, inventions, encounters – they explore molecular, psychotropic, and derivative aesthetics. They participated in documenta fifteen and the 49th Venice Biennale (Austrian Pavilion), among other major exhibitions, and their work has been shown at the New Museum New York, Kunstinstituut Melly (formerly Witte de With), and Kunsthalle St. Gallen.

**Irma Markulin** completed her education at the Academy of Fine Arts in Zagreb and the Weißensee Academy of Art in Berlin, among other institutions. She works with images that are anchored in the collective memory, using painterly means to examine their staging in different political contexts. Markulin's works have been shown at numerous exhibitions at home and abroad, and she has received several international art scholarships, most recently Culture Moves Europe (2024/25) and a scholarship from the Croatian Ministry of Culture and Media (2023).

**Helga Paris** (1938 Gollnow, Pomerania – 2024 Berlin) plays a prominent role in German photography. She is considered a chronicler of the post-war period in East Germany, having photographed people and everyday life in East German cities over several decades. With few exceptions and without formal training, she worked exclusively on her own initiative, since there was no market for her work in the GDR. Nevertheless, her work was extremely popular, even during the GDR era. Her photographs have been shown internationally in exhibitions and publications. In 2019, the artist donated her negative archive to the Academy of Arts in Berlin, of which she had been a member since 1996.

**A. R. Penck** (Ralf Winkler, 1939 Dresden – 2017 Zurich) was a painter, draftsman, sculptor, graphic artist, Super 8 filmmaker, musician, and author. In his life and artistic practice, he combined analytical and visual thinking with ideas from philosophy, natural science, information theory, and technology. In 1980, Penck was forced to leave the GDR and moved to the Federal Republic of Germany. Penck was a protagonist of 'Junge Wilde' (Young Wild Ones), as well as one of the most important artistic chroniclers of recent German history. His works can be found in collections such as the Museum Ludwig, the Museum of Modern Art, and the Kunstmuseum Den Haag.

**Ramona Schacht and Luca Bublik** combine artistic and social science research in their joint practice. For several years, they have been working with archives and image collections that document work in the GDR and the Soviet Union. Schacht studied photography at the Academy of Visual Arts Leipzig under Heidi Specker, and received the Wüstenrot Foundation's Documentary Photography Award (2023/24) as well as the Museum der bildenden Künste Leipzig Connect Award (2018). Her work has been exhibited at Urbane Künste Ruhr and Das Minsk, Potsdam, among other venues. Luca Bublik received his doctorate from the Bauhaus University Weimar, and works as a freelance author and curator. Most recently, he participated artistically in Urbane Künste Ruhr 2025 and curated the exhibition *Reading the Spinnerei* on Rita Große's work and industrial photography at the Archiv Massiv Leipzig.

**Sandra Schäfer**'s work in film, photography, and artistic research focuses on the processes of creating urban and transregional spaces, history, and image politics. In 2018, she completed her artistic PhD on militant images and space politics at the Hochschule für bildende Künste Hamburg. Schäfer is a professor at the Academy of Fine Arts in Munich and an associate member of the feminist film distributor Cinenova in London. Her work is regularly shown at festivals such as the 66th and 67th Berlinale (Forum Expanded), Berlin, and at exhibitions in Germany and abroad. She has published numerous books with publishers including Archive Books, Camera Austria, and Spector Books.

**Suzanne Treister** initially worked as a painter before becoming a pioneer in the field of digital media and the internet in the early 1990s. She uses various media such as video, drawing, and watercolour to explore the relationship between new technologies, alternative belief systems and the future of humanity. With speculative reinterpretations of history, she examines the existence of hidden forces at work in the world. Her work has been exhibited at numerous institutions, including the Tate Modern, the 14th Shanghai Biennale (2023), and the Centre Pompidou.

**Werner Tübke** (1929 Schönbeck, Elbe – 2004 Leipzig) was a co-founder of the Leipzig School. After completing an apprenticeship as a painter, he studied at the art academies in Leipzig and Greifswald. He is known for his painting style in the tradition of the Renaissance and Mannerism. From the early 1970s onwards, Tübke enjoyed international success, with museums in Germany and abroad acquiring his paintings. His monumental *Peasants' War Panorama* in Bad Frankenhausen was completed in 1989.

**Marion Wenzel** studied photography at the Academy of Visual Arts in Leipzig under Prof. Evelyn Richter. Inspired by her professor, she began photographing the open-cast mines in the south of Leipzig in the early 1980s. Over several decades, she created an archive that reveals the man-made changes to the landscape and the environmental destruction that accompanied it. From 2005 to 2025, Wenzel worked as a collection photographer for the University of Leipzig, documenting the university's history in numerous photographs, including the removal of the Karl Marx relief, the demolition of the socialist campus buildings, and the construction of the Paulinum.

**Ruth Wolf-Rehfeldt** (1932 Wurzen – 2024 Berlin) created a diverse oeuvre of paintings, drawings, collages, and so-called typewritings. In these works, created with a typewriter on paper, she combined poetry, graphic design, and conceptual art. Together with her partner, Robert Rehfeldt, she was part of the international mail art movement in the GDR, which facilitated international artistic exchange and the uncensored dissemination of art and ideas. After 1989, Wolf-Rehfeldt completely ceased her artistic work. Her work has been exhibited widely, including at Das Minsk and at documenta 14, and is represented in collections such as the Bundeskunstsammlung and the Museum Ludwig. In 2022, she was awarded the Hannah Höch Prize.

## Bibliography, essay

Gerhard Barkleit, *Mikroelektronik in der DDR. SED, Staatsapparat und Staatssicherheit im Wettstreit der Systeme* (Dresden: Hannah-Ahrend-Institut, 2000)

Michel Foucault, 'Return to History', in: James D. Faubion (ed.), *Aesthetics, Method, and Epistemology* (New York: The New Press, 1998)

Robert Havemann, *Morgen. Die Industriegesellschaft am Scheideweg. Kritik und reale Utopie* (München, Zürich: Piper, 1980)

Hans-Hermann Hertle, 'Vor dem Bankrott der DDR. Dokumente des Politbüros des ZK der SED aus dem Jahre 1988 zum Scheitern der "Einheit von Wirtschafts- und Sozialpolitik. Die Schürer/Mittag-Kontroverse"' (Berlin: Berliner Arbeitshefte und Berichte der sozial-wissenschaftlichen Forschung, 1991)

Roman Jakobson, *Semiotik. Ausgewählte Texte 1919–1982* (Frankfurt am Main: Suhrkamp, 1992)

Georg Klaus, *Kybernetik und Erkenntnistheorie* (Berlin: VEB Deutscher Verlag der Wissenschaften, 1972)

Ilko-Sascha Kowalczuk, *Walter Ulbricht. Der kommunistische Diktator* (München: C.H. Beck, 2024)

Olaf Klenke, *Ist die DDR an der Globalisierung gescheitert? Autarke Wirtschaftspolitik versus internationale Weltwirtschaft – Das Beispiel Mikroelektronik* (Frankfurt am Main et al.: Peter Lang. Europäischer Verlag der Wissenschaften, 2001)

Olaf Klenke, *Kampfauftrag Mikrochip. Rationalisierung und sozialer Konflikt in der DDR* (Hamburg: VSA-Verlag, 2008)

Johannes Müller, *Grundlagen der Systematischen Heuristik* (Berlin: Dietz Verlag, 1970)

Johannes Müller, *Arbeitsmethoden der Technik-wissenschaften. Systematik, Heuristik, Kreativität* (Berlin et al.: Springer Verlag, 1990)

Simon Nagy, *Zeit abschaffen. Ein hauntologischer Essay gegen die Arbeit, die Familie und die Herrschaft der Zeit* (Münster: Unrast Verlag, 2024)

Andrew Pickering, *Kybernetik und Neue Ontologie* (Berlin: Merve Verlag, 2007)

I. A. Poletajew, *Kybernetik. Kurze Einführung in eine neue Wissenschaft*, published by Georg Klaus (Berlin: VEB Deutscher Verlag der Wissenschaften, 1962)

Annegret Schüle, *BWS Sömmerda. Die wechselvolle Geschichte eines Industriestandortes in Thüringen. 1816–1995* (Erfurt: DESOTRON Verlagsgesellschaft, 1995)

Gerhard Schürer, *Gewagt und verloren. Eine deutsche Biografie* (Frankfurt (Oder): Frankfurter Oder Editionen, 1996)

Silicon Saxony e.V., *Silicon Saxony. Die Story* (Dresden: Edition JS Dresden, 2006)

Erich Sobeslavsky, Nikolaus Joachim Lehmann, *Zur Geschichte von Rechentechnik und Datenverarbeitung in der DDR 1946-1968* (Dresden: Hannah-Ahrend-Institut, 1996)

Oliver Sukrow, *Arbeit. Wohnen. Computer. Zur Utopie in der bildenden Kunst und Architektur der DDR in den 1960er Jahren* (Heidelberg: University Publishing, 2018)

Tiqqun, *Kybernetik und Revolte* (Zürich: Diaphanes, 2024)

Sergej Tretjakow, *Die Arbeit des Schriftstellers. Aufsätze, Reportagen, Porträts* (Reinbeck bei Hamburg: Rowohlt Taschenbuch, 1972)

Manfred Tumma, Hans Bader, Lothar Schreier, *Von Mercedes zu Robotron. Ein Bilderbuch der besonderen Art* (Zella-Mehlis/Meinnigen: Heinrich-Jung-Verlags-gesellschaft, 2008)

Norbert Wiener, *Mensch und Menschmaschine, Kybernetik und Gesellschaft* (Frankfurt am Main: Athenäum Verlag, 1964)

Robert-Havemann-Gesellschaft, '06.08.1989 "Bringt uns nicht Silizi-um" Proteste gegen den Bau eines Reinstsiliziumwerks in Dresden-Gittersee', https://www.havemann-gesellschaft.de/06081989-bringtuns-nicht-silizi-um-proteste-gegen-den-bau-einesreinstsiliziumwerks-in-dresden-gittersee/. [accessed:14 January 2026]

## List of works in the exhibition

### Karl-Heinz Adler

Serial lines, shifted vertically
1967/68 | Drawing, graphite on cardboard | 64×64 cm

Serial lines, shifted diagonally
1968 | 2 drawings, graphite on cardboard | 64×64 cm

6 layered rectangles, tilted upwards at the centre
1984 | Relief, collage on paper | 40×26 cm

Design variant for a partly open sculptural partition wall, Cottbus (A) (modular system of concrete blocks)
Early 1970s | Letterpress printing, collage on cardboard | 25×38.3 cm

Design for a light column (modular system of concrete blocks, not executed)
1977 | Letterpress printing, collage, pen, cardboard | 38.5×35.5 cm

Design variant for a sculptural partition wall, Cottbus (A) (modular system of concrete blocks)
Early 1970s | Letterpress printing, collage on cardboard | 25×74 cm

Galerie EIGEN+ART Leipzig/Berlin

### Tina Bara

BUNA eine Zeit (BUNA A Time)
1988/2025 | Video, b/w, sound | 40 min
  Concept, camera, editing: Tina Bara
  Music: Nino Sandow
  Text, sound: Tina Bara
  Narrator: Tina Bara, Hermann Beyer
  Translation: Louise Bromby
  Postproduction, subtitles: Kante Film
  Song and text citations:
    Lew Oschanin, *Lied von der unruhevollen Jugend*, 1958
    Bertolt Brecht, Hans Eisler, *Einheitsfrontlied*, 1934, English translation H.R. Hays
    Bertolt Brecht, *Psalm: Wir haben nicht mit den Lidern geblinzelt*, 1920
    Bertolt Brecht, *Vom Schwimmen in Seen und Flüssen*, 1919, English translation H.R. Hays
    Gerhart Hauptmann, *Dorothea Angermann*, 1925

BUNA eine Zeit – Nachtrag (BUNA A Time – Epilogue)
2025 | Video, colour, sound | 20 min | Photographic wallpaper
  Camera, editing: Tina Bara
  Music: Nino Sandow
  Translation: Louise Bromby
  Postproduction, subtitles: Kante Film

GfZK Collection

### Horst Bartnig

3622 Variationen (3622 Variations)
1984/85 | Computer-generated graphics, hand-printed line etching | 4 sheets, 94.5×74.5 cm

GfZK Collection

### Nadja Buttendorf

Robotron – a tech opera
HD video, 3D animation, 4K, colour, sound
  Season 01 | 2018 | 9:18 min
  Season 02 | 2019 | 6:45 min
  Season 4K (aka Season 03) | 2020 | 1:55 min
  Season 3D (aka Season 04) | 2021 | 11:00 min

www.youtube.com/watch?v=SAVEQbWXwzs&list=PL qjlSv13g0qpdLOaAL-0-J_BtZPHHEUmw

rosie
2025 | Word mark (design: David Polzin), pyjamas, sleep mask, excerpt from the workers' company newspaper of VEB Robotron-Elektronik Dresden and VEB Robotron Projekt Dresden, 14 February 1990, no.3/90, last page | Dimensions variable

### Carlfriedrich Claus

Konjunktionen, Einheit und Kampf der Gegensätze in Landschaft, bezogen auf das kommunistische Zukunftsproblem: Naturalisierung des Menschen, Humanisierung der Natur (Conjunctions, Unity and Conflict of Opposites in Landscape, related to the Communist Problem of the Future: Naturalization of Humans, Humanization of Nature)
1968 | Drawing on both sides of transparent paper 20.5×29.1 cm

Studie zu Gedanken-Fingerbewegungen (Study on Thought-Induced Finger Movements)
1971 | Pen and black and blue ink, manual blurrings on transparent paper, drawings on both sides | 14.5×20.8 cm

durchgang durch sich 63 phasen (passage through the self 63 phases)
1959 | Typescript, typewriter on carbon paper and 66 sheets of carbon copy paper | 21 ×15 cm

GfZK Collection

### Karl Clauss Dietel
### Georg Eckelt

B/w photographs, exhibition copies

Work photographs taken during the design process for the Robotron mainframe computer, photographer unknown
1964 | 11×11 cm

Elements of the Robotron R300 mainframe computer, model, photographed by Georg Eckelt
1964 | 18×24 cm

The Robotron R300 mainframe computer in factories and data centres, photographer unknown | 18×24 cm

Kunstsammlungen Chemnitz, archival material from the estate of Karl Clauss Dietel

### Antye Guenther

Operation ZWIEBELMUSTER (Operation Blue Onion)
2021–25 | Coffee service, Meissen porcelain, 28 pieces; blue Onion pattern with partially multi-layered platinum overglaze; six unique pieces with a modified Blue Onion design based on the artist's drawings; documents; 1-megabit chip layout plan; performance with image and research material | Dimensions variable

### Margret Hoppe

Leben im Sozialismus – Datenverarbeitung, VEB Robotron (Life in Socialism – Data Processing, VEB Robotron)
2012 | 4 C-Prints | 30×40 cm
  Arno Rink, Wall Painting in the Robotron Building 1970, Leipzig
  Frank Ruddigkeit, Wall Painting in the Robotron Building 1970, Leipzig
  Rolf Kuhrt, Wall Painting in the Robotron Building 1970, Leipzig
  Klaus Schwabe, Wall Painting in the Robotron Building 1970, Leipzig

Die verschwundenen Bilder, Werner Tübke, Arbeiterklasse und Intelligenz 1973, Mischtechnik, Universität Leipzig (The Missing Paintings, Werner Tübke, Working Class and Intelligentsia 1973, mixed media, Leipzig University)
2006 | C-Print | 125×100 cm

### Su Yu Hsin

Particular Waters
2023 | Video, colour, sound | 18:38 min
  Director, editor, writer: Su Yu Hsin
  Production coordinator: Wade Cherng
  Cinematographer: Yuro Huang
  Boom operator: Chen Yung
  2nd sound operator: Chen Yi-Zhen
  Sound design: Yun Fang Tseng
  Sound mix: Jochen Jezussek
  Performer: Wu Yu Hsin, Chen Yung
  Narration recording: Wei Yu Chung, Don Yo
  Colour grading: Mel Rico
  Edit advice: Clemens von Wedemeyer, Mareike Bernien
  Field research consultant: Prof. Ya-Chung Chuang
  Field trip guide: Ramus Tai

Where Clouds Once Formed
2025 | Video, colour, sound | 13:35 min
    Inspiration and quotes: Ofelia Zepeda,
        *Na:nko Ma:s Cewagī / Cloud Song*
    Director, editor, writer: Su Yu Hsin
    Local field producer: Chloe Yintzu Huang
    Cinematographer: Yuro Huang
    Boom operator: Chloe Yintzu Huang, Su Yu Hsin
    Local fixer: Jo-Ting Hsu
    Sound design: Yun Fang Tseng
    Sound mix: Jochen Jezussek
    Voice actress: Julia Rodríguez
    Narration recording: fünften Jens Tröndle
    Colour grading: Mel Rico
    Edit advice: Clemens von Wedemeyer

Sunshine-belt Machine
2026 | Video, colour, sound | 14:00 min
    Director, editor, writer: Su Yu Hsin
    Local field producer: Kathrin Lemcke
    Cinematographer: Jonas Matauschek
    Boom operator: Nadine Rangosch, Su Yu Hsin
    Sound design: Peter Hermans, Yun Fang Tseng
    Sound mix: Jochen Jezussek
    Voice-over: Su Yu Hsin
    Narration recording: Daniel Chen,
        fünften Jens Tröndle
    Colour grading: Mel Rico
    Archival sources:
        Senckenberg Naturhistorische Sammlungen
            Dresden
        Betriebssammlung des Steinkohlewerks/
            Bergbaubetriebs Willi Agatz
        Regionale Mineraliensammlung Sachsen
        Sammlung Paläobotanik
        Sächsisches Landesamt für Umwelt,
            Landwirtschaft und Geologie
        TU Bergakademie Freiberg Kustodie
        Sammlung Nichteisenmetallurgie
        Silicon wafers with inscriptions 40 years of suc-
            cessful class struggle and the view of the historic
            Alte Elisabeth mine
        Robert-Havemann-Gesellschaft e.V.
            Archiv der DDR-Opposition
        Wismut GmbH Archiv
        Lageplan – Gesamtbebauungsplan
            Reinstsiliziumwerk Gittersee
        Silitronic AG Archiv
        rbb media GmbH

**Francis Hunger**

Statistical Hypnagogia
2021 | Sound installation in the courtyard; video,
colour, sound | 12:26 min

**knowbotiq**

Clean Room affect.aliens
2025 | Glove boxes made from recycled agricultural
films, e-papers, PVC pipes, Raspberry Pi, tab
Dimensions variable
    Sound: Pablo Torres

**Irma Markulin**

Biography beyond Statistics
2022 | B/w photographs, perforated | 56×56 cm
    Photos: Ulrich Häßler, Wolfgang Thieme,
        Federal Archives

**Helga Paris**

Leipzig Hauptbahnhof (Leipzig Central Station)
1981–82/2025 | Exhibition copies, digital
prints | 24×33 cm

Estate Helga Paris

**A. R. Penck**

Skizze zu Weltbild Nr. 4 (Sketch for Worldview No. 4)
1962, painted over in the 1970s | Latex over ink on
cardboard, mounted on canvas | 95.5×75.5 cm

Computermodell (Computer Model)
1970 | Fiber pen in blue and red | 29.8×42.2 cm

From the series: 20 Skizzen von 1968
(20 Sketches from 1968)
1968 | Blue ink on cardboard | 5/20: 20×14.4 cm
9/20: 16.9×14.6 cm | 13/20: 17.1×14.7 cm
15/20: 16.1×14.4 cm | 19/20: 14.1×11.8 cm

Städtische Galerie Dresden – Kunstsammlung,
Museen der Stadt Dresden, *Skizze zu Weltbild Nr. 4*
and *Computermodell* acquired with the support of
the Ostdeutsche Sparkassenstiftung im Freistaat
Sachsen together with Ostsächsische Sparkasse
Dresden

**Ramona Schacht and Luca Bublik with Rita Große**

Niewidzialne Pracownice (Invisible workers) – Polish
women in the GDR's semiconductor production
2025 | Leaflet; fine art prints in a multi-piece wooden
frame, text | 190×160 cm
    Source images: private archive Rita Große, Leipzig

**Sandra Schäfer**

Where Gravity Fades
2025 | Video, colour, sound | 19:55 min
Room construction made of wood, wire sculptures
Dimensions variable
    Dramaturgy: Janina Herhoffer
    Performers: C. Bain, Jyl Franzbecker,
        Annegret Schalke
    Camera: Bernadette Paaßen
    Sound: Manuela Schininá
    Set design: Àngela Ribera
    Sound design: Steffen Martin
    Sound mixing: Jochen Jezussek
    Colour grading: Till Beckmann
    Graphic design: Wolfgang Schwärzler
    Research assistance: Sirrah Hamann
    Line producer: Jyl Franzbecker with Mizu Sugai
    Catering: Clelia Villarreal
    Set-up: Josephin Hanke, Tina Steiger, Erwin Weber,
        Ping-Zsiang Wang
    Film footage of coal mining: Jochen Balke
    Music:
        Foam and Sand (Robert Koch) and Midori Hirano,
            *Circle 19 – Midori Hirano Rework*, 2021,
            Erased Tapes Music
        CoH and Midori Hirano, *Flowers of Gravity*, 2025,
            Licensed courtesy of Mind Travels Series / Ici,
            d'ailleurs, Erased Tapes Music
    Additional research & interviews:
        Stephan Moitra, Dörthe Schmidt, Sophia Sievers,
            Pauline Oemler
        German Mining Museum
        Ann Michelle van Achterberg and Ulf Tjåland
        Magma Geopark, Norway
        Lars Raymond Sondresden
        Titania AS, Norway
    Text fragments:
        Frank B. Gilbreth, *Motion Study, a Method for
            Increasing the Efficiency of the Workman*, 1921
        Aleksei Kapitonovich Gastev, *Order 2 & 5*, 1921
        Thorsten Günther, Jörg Werner, *Interviews with
            Former Mining Workers*, 2025
        United Nations, *Treaty on Principles Governing the
            Activities of States in the Exploration and Use
            of Outer Space, including the Moon and Other
            Celestial Bodies*, 1967

**Suzanne Treister**

HEXEN 5.0 / Historical Diagrams
2023–25 | Ink on paper, digital print | Dimensions
variable
    Main Diagram
    From the Golem via Deep Learning to Machine
        Colonisation of the Multiverse
    From Surveillance Capitalism via New
        Countercultures of Refusal to Web 5.0 and
        Decentralised Autonomous Futures
    From the Potential Destruction of the Universe
        via Interplanetary Ecosystems and Psychedelic
        Spaceships to Astrocognition
    From Mass Extinctions via The Climate Crisis to
        Cybernetic Ecosystems and Spiritual Earth System
        Science towards a Return to a Self-Regulating
        Planet
    From Science Fiction via Traditional Knowledge
        Systems and Global Futurisms to Ethical
        MetaUtopias

Concerning Technological Histories of Socialist
Computing as Instruments for Collective Progress,
Economic Planning, Education, State Coordination
and Repression
2025 | Ink on paper, digital print | Dimensions variable

**Werner Tübke**

Arbeiterklasse und Intelligenz
(Working Class and Intelligentsia)
1970–73 | Mural | 270×1380 cm

In der Meßwarte (In the Control Room)
Preliminary study for Working Class and Intelligentsia
1970 | Graphite on paper | 24.3×29 cm

Kunstbesitz/Kustodie der Universität Leipzig

Sketch for Working Class and Intelligentsia
1971 | Tempera on canvas | 2 pieces, 130×260 cm

Rechenzentrum (Computation Centre)
Preliminary study for Working Class and Intelligentsia
1971 | Graphite on paper | 65.8×95 cm

In der Meßwarte (In the Control Room)
Preliminary study for Working Class and Intelligentsia
1970 | Graphite on paper | 24.3×29 cm

Estate Werner Tübke, Galerie Schwind

**Marion Wenzel**

Pleinair Mikroelektronik Frankfurt (Oder)
1989 | Baryte prints | Various sizes, ca 40 × 60 cm

Museum Utopie und Alltag (Bestand Beeskow)

**Ruth Wolf-Rehfeldt**

Hommage à Shannon
1972 | Carbon copy | 29.5×21 cm

ChertLüdde, Berlin

Planet
1970s | Zincography | 21×15 cm

Wachstum (Growth)
1970s | Zincography | 21×14.5 cm

Evolution
1972 | Zincography | 21×15 cm

Spheres of Interest
1979 | Zincography | 21.5×30 cm

Information (Informationsbildung)
1970s | Zincography | 14.5×10.5 cm

Wucherungen (Convexities)
1970s | Zincography | 21×14.5 cm

Zeichenraum
1970s | Zincography | 10.5×14.5 cm

Zeichenräume
1970s | Zincography | 10.5×14.5 cm

Zeichenraum 8
1979 | Zincography | 10.5×14.5 cm

Zeichenräume 11
1979 | Zincography | 10.5×14.5 cm

Cagy Being I
1980 | Zincography | 29.5×21 cm

Steps to Heaven (Steps to the Stars)
1981 | Zincography | 31×21.5 cm

Cages on the Run
1980s | Zincography | 21×15 cm

GfZK Collection

## Exhibition

Robotron. Code and Utopia
25.10.2025–22.2.2026
GfZK–Museum of Contemporary Art Leipzig

Robotron. Working Class and Intelligentsia
14.3.–26.7.2026
HMKV Hartware MedienKunstVerein Dortmund

With: Karl-Heinz Adler, Tina Bara, Horst Bartnig, Nadja Buttendorf, Carlfriedrich Claus, Karl Clauss Dietel, Georg Eckelt, Antye Guenther, Margret Hoppe, Su Yu Hsin, Francis Hunger, knowbotiq, Irma Markulin, Helga Paris, A.R. Penck, Ramona Schacht and Luca Bublik with Rita Große, Sandra Schäfer, Suzanne Treister, Werner Tübke, Marion Wenzel, Ruth Wolf-Rehfeldt

Curatorial Team: Inke Arns (HMKV), Sabine Weier (GfZK), Jan Wenzel (Spector Books), Mathias Wittmann (HMKV), Franciska Zólyom (GfZK)
Project Management: Hanar Hupka, Constance Künzel (until March 2025)
Graphic Design: Wolfgang Schwärzler
Scenography: Julia Gerke
English translation: Louise Bromby, Alisa Kotmair

Initiated by: Jochen Becker
Research: Tim Tetzner (until January 2025)

GfZK
Director, Curator: Franciska Zólyom
Head of Office: Annett Koch
Administrative Manager, Sustainability Officer: Julia Eckert
Head of Art Mediation: Alexandra Friedrich, Lena Seik
Art Mediation: Nora Krings
Depot Manager, Exhibition Technician: Lars Bergmann
Press and Public Relations, Editor: Sabine Weier
Marketing, Event Management: Julia Gollan
Curatorial Assistant: Hanar Hupka
Librarian: Nicole Döll
Building Services: Marcel Fichtner, Hans Thiele
System Administrator: Lars Eidam
Fellow of the Cultural Foundation of the Free State of Saxony: Simon Kurti
Interns: Soraya Bautz, Pia Brand, Christina Heindl, Emilia Schulz
Mediation Team: Mina Bamarni, Martin Haufe, Alexandra Ivanciu, Daniela Junghans, Genesis Kahveci, Saori Kaneko, Tania Kolbe, Romy Kroppe, Johanna Krümpelbeck, Matilda Materni, Melanie Ruhe, Linus Saternus, Wiebke Steinert, Victor Stinglhamber, Hanna Thuma, Eduardo Xerez
Technical Team: Morten Bjerre, Alicia Franzke, Julia Gerke (Head), Loïc Martin, Paul Nägele, Valentina Plank, Marie Seelen, Julius Vogelsberg

HMKV
Director: Dr. Inke Arns
Managing Director: Mathias Wittmann
Technical Director: Stephan Karass
Exhibition Management: Mareen Biermann, Luise Klonowski, Anna Daschkewitz
Communication: Lisa Demant, David Kleinekottmann, Ann-Katrin Drews
Cultural Education: Linda Beckmann
Assistant Commercial Administration: Katharina Priestley
Consultant for Finance, Accounting and Controlling: Simone Czech
Economic Business and Sustainability Management: Kathleen Ansorg
Director of Operations: Linda Richerd
Info Team: Lisa-Marie Ayomide Ademola, Evelyn Hennor, Naomi Hennor, Mathis Jüres, Silvia Liebig, Steven Natusch, Richard Opoku-Agyemang, Sarah Ruholl, Cornelius Stiegemann, Belisa Vazquez-Henneken, Sophia Weber
IT Technician: Daniel Veselka
Installation Team: Sanja Biere, Ulvis Müller, Mark Drückler, Zeljko Petonjic

## Imprint

Editors: Inke Arns, Sabine Weier, Jan Wenzel, Franciska Zólyom

Essay: Jan Wenzel
Artist texts: Inke Arns, Sabine Weier, Franciska Zólyom
Interviews:
Susanne Altmann: Hanar Hupka, Sabine Weier
Regina Bittner: Sabine Weier, Franciska Zólyom
Rita Große: Hanar Hupka, Sabine Weier
Rolf Heinemann: Bundesstifung Aufarbeitung
Francis Hunger: Sabine Weier, Jan Wenzel
Jens Knobloch: Antye Guenther
Thomas Kübler: Sabine Weier
Henrike Voigtländer: Sabine Weier

Editorial: Hanar Hupka, Sabine Weier, Jan Wenzel, Franciska Zólyom
Editing: Jan-Frederik Bandel, Sabine Weier
English translation: Louise Bromby, Sonja Hornung, Alisa Kotmair
Proofreading: Louise Bromby
Design: Wolfgang Schwärzler
Image processing: Carsten Humme
Printing and Processing: Gutenberg Beuys Feindruckerei GmbH
Paper: Joly Colors Rosa 80/230 g/m², Magno Volumne 80/250 g/m², Speed Gloss 90 g/m²
Typefaces: Friedl (Camelot Typefaces), Lector (Forgotten Shapes), Robotron24 (WS)

Published by:
Spector Books
Harkortstraße 10
D-04107 Leipzig, Germany
www.spectorbooks.com

© 2026 the editors, authors, artists, GfZK–Museum for Contemporary Art Leipzig, HMKV Hartware MedienKunstVerein e.V., Spector Books

All rights reserved

Reproduction (in whole or in part) only with explicit permission

Installation views: Alexandra Ivanciu (6, 8, 81–84), Marion Wenzel (22)

Image reproduction: A. Herrmann (77), humme (15–17, 19, 20, 36–38, 49–52, 71–74), PUNCTUM/Bertram Kober (9–12), Martin Reich (92, 93), Uwe Walter (27–32), Marion Wenzel (21–22), Franz Zadnicek (35)

© VG Bild-Kunst, Bonn, 2026 for the works of

Carlfriedrich Claus, Karl Clauss Dietel, Francis Hunger, Margret Hoppe, Rolf Kuhrt, Irma Markulin, A.R. Penck, Arno Rink, Frank Ruddigkeit, Ramona Schacht, Sandra Schäfer, Klaus Schwabe, Werner Tübke

Claims pursuant to § 60H URHG (German Copyright Act) for the reproduction of images of the exhibits/works are asserted by VG Bild-Kunst, Bonn.

ISBN: 978-3-95905-953-4

First edition

Distribution:
Germany, Austria: GVA, Gemeinsame Verlagsauslieferung Göttingen GmbH & Co. KG, www.gva-verlage.de
Switzerland: AVA Verlagsauslieferung AG, www.ava.ch
France, Belgium: Interart Paris, www.interart.fr
UK: Central Books Ltd, www.centralbooks.com
USA, Canada, Central and South America, Africa: ARTBOOK/D.A.P., www.artbook.com
South Korea: The Book Society, www.thebooksociety.org
Japan: twelvebooks, www.twelve-books.com
Australia, New Zealand: Perimeter Distribution, www.perimeterdistribution.com

This publication is also available in German:
ISBN: 978-3-95905-952-7

## Responsible parties

Stiftung Galerie für Zeitgenössische Kunst Leipzig
Register-Nr. 6/2002
Karl-Tauchnitz-Str. 9–11
D-04107 Leipzig
Tel: +49 341 140 81–0
E-Mail: office@gfzk.de
www.gfzk.de

and

Hartware MedienKunstVerein e.V.
VR 4833, Ust ID NR.: DE 268698763
Executive Board: Stefan Hilterhaus, Dr. Inke Arns
At Dortmunder U, Ebene 3
Leonie-Reygers-Terrasse
D-44137 Dortmund
Office: Park der Partnerstädte 2, D-44137 Dortmund
Tel: +49 231 13 73 21–55
E-Mail: info@hmkv.de
www.hmkv.de

## Funding

Funded by the Kulturstiftung des Bundes (German Federal Cultural Foundation). Funded by the Beauftragter der Bundesregierung für Kultur und Medien (Federal Government Commissioner for Culture and the Media). Funded by Ostdeutsche Sparkassenstiftung with Sparkasse Leipzig. knowbotiq is supported by Pro Helvetia. Sandra Schäfer is supported by Medienboard Berlin-Brandenburg.


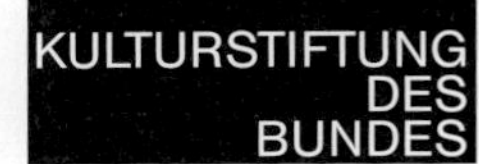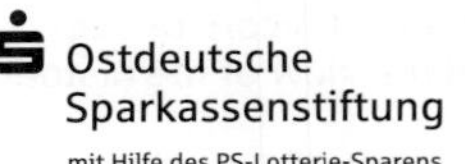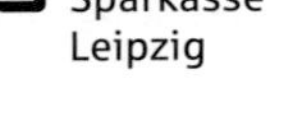

Media partners GfZK:

Media partner HMKV:

The project Robotron. Code and Utopia / Working Class and Intelligentsia is a collaboration between GfZK–Museum of Contemporary Art and HMKV Hartware MedienKunstVerein Dortmund.

The Foundation Galerie für Zeitgenössische Kunst Leipzig is supported by the City of Leipzig, the Free State of Saxony (SMWK), and the Friends of the GfZK Leipzig. It is partly financed through public funds on the basis of the budget approved by the members of the Landtag of the Free State of Saxony.

The HMKV is funded by the Ministry of Culture and Science of the State of North Rhine-Westphalia, the city of Dortmund, and the Dortmunder U.